CLUSTER DEVELOPMENT AND POLICY

Other titles in the collection

Transition, Cohesion and Regional Policy
in Central and Eastern Europe
Edited by John Bachtler, Ruth Downes and Grzegorz Gorzelak

Policy Competition and
Foreign Direct Investment in Europe
Edited by Philip Raines and Ross Brown

Cluster Development and Policy

Edited by
PHILIP RAINES
European Policies Research Centre
University of Strathclyde, UK

Routledge
Taylor & Francis Group

LONDON AND NEW YORK

First published 2002 by Ashgate Publishing

Reissued 2018 by Routledge
2 Park Square, Milton Park, Abingdon, Oxon OX14 4RN
711 Third Avenue, New York, NY 10017, USA

Routledge is an imprint of the Taylor & Francis Group, an informa business

Publisher's Note
The publisher has gone to great lengths to ensure the quality of this reprint but points out that some imperfections in the original copies may be apparent.

Disclaimer
The publisher has made every effort to trace copyright holders and welcomes correspondence from those they have been unable to contact.

A Library of Congress record exists under LC control number: 2002018638

ISBN 13: 978-1-138-71764-0 (hbk)
ISBN 13: 978-1-138-71763-3 (pbk)
ISBN 13: 978-1-315-19625-1 (ebk)

Contents

PART 3: CONCLUSIONS

List of Figures and Tables

Figures

Tables

Preface

The following report is principally based on a study conducted by the European Policies Research Centre of the University of Strathclyde in Glasgow. Funded by several European regional development organisations, the *Euro-Cluster* project aimed to identify and understand the key factors behind the successful design and delivery of cluster development policies. Fieldwork consisted of face-to-face interviews with the main policy-making participants in each area and analysis of associated strategies, evaluations and documents. The research team consisted of the following:

- Philip Raines (Senior Research Fellow, European Policies Research Centre, University of Strathclyde, Glasgow, UK)
- Peter Ache (Visiting Professor, TU Hamburg-Harburg, Hamburg, Germany)
- François Josserand (Researcher, EPRC)
- Mary Louise Rooney (Research Fellow, EPRC)
- Sandra Taylor (Research Fellow, EPRC)

In addition, Christian Hartmann (Researcher, InTeReg, Joanneum Research, Graz, Austria) provided the case-study chapter on Styria.

The research team is grateful to the *Euro-Cluster* sponsors for their support: Enterprise Ireland (Ireland); Scottish Enterprise (UK); the Scottish Executive (UK); the Northern Ireland Department of Enterprise, Trade and Industry (UK) the Welsh Development Agency (UK); the Ministry of Local Government and Regional Development (Norway); the East Sweden Development Agency (Sweden); and the Council of Tampere Region (Finland).

Lastly, the authors of the study wish to acknowledge Moira Lowe of EPRC for the thankless task of formatting the book for publication.

Philip Raines
EPRC
Glasgow

Chapter 1

Introduction

Philip Raines

Few phenomena have marked discussion of economic development in recent years so much as the interest shown in the 'cluster' concept. Publicised by the work of Michael Porter and others, the proliferation of work on clusters and cluster-based policies points to one of the most dynamic exchanges between economic development theory and practice for several decades (Porter, 1990a; Held, 1996; Rosenfeld, 1997; Steiner, 1998; OECD, 1999; den Hertog, Bergman and Charles, 2001; Mariussen, 2001). As a result, there is a growing, widespread belief among policy-makers worldwide that clusters can form the basis of a successful economic strategy by supporting regional innovation, encouraging technological spillovers, producing economies of scale and scope and enhancing self-sustaining local economic development. At the same time, questions have been raised about whether the theoretical underpinnings and policy applications of the cluster approach are little more than 'old wine in new bottles', not so much borrowing from as re-labelling existing ideas. Nevertheless, whether hailed as a critical shift in policy understanding or criticised as a false panacea, it is difficult to deny that the approach to cluster development and policy represents a uniquely vigorous interaction between the academic and policy-making spheres.

Although definitions vary, clusters can be thought of as networks of firms, research institutes and public bodies, which tend to be located in relatively close geographical proximity and whose cross-sectoral linkages generate and renew local competitive advantage. In this, the cluster concept is not immediately novel. In economic development literature, the fundamental links between economic agglomeration and competitiveness are long-standing, dating back to Alfred Marshall in the late 19th century (Marshall, 1961), if not earlier. Studies of successful regional economies over the past few decades have regularly uncovered elements of clustering, ranging from the local webs of small, crafts-based enterprises in the northern Italian industrial districts to the international concentration of high-technology companies in Silicon Valley, from competitive networks of agro-businesses in the rural regions of Denmark to web design and multimedia firms in New York city.

Nonetheless, discussion of the validity and implications of the cluster concept has introduced two key important elements into economic development. First, it has brought together a series of earlier and parallel debates – including those relating to 'industrial districts', 'regional innovation systems' and 'learning regions' – and promoted a wider discussion of the sources of local competitive advantage. In this respect, the ambiguity of the cluster concept – often cited as a weakness – has surprisingly allowed a range of different economic development ideas to be combined in new configurations. It has not only raised interest in these ideas but helped to sharpen understanding of them.

Second, the policy implications of the cluster approach have been an integral part of the debate. While the role of policy intervention has only been discussed in economic development literature more fully in recent years, interest by the policy-making community in cluster development has been both intensive and pervasive. Over the last few years, there has been a dramatic proliferation of policies designed to promote development of clusters of firms and industries (or at least, purport to) (Enright, 2000). In Europe alone, cluster-based policies can already be found at national, regional and local levels in Austria, Belgium, Denmark, Finland, France, Germany, Italy, the Netherlands, Spain, Sweden and the UK (case-study examples of seven of these are presented in this volume) and are in preparation in several other countries. Indeed, the annual cluster-related conferences organised by both DATAR and the OECD as well as the Competitiveness Institute have regularly attracted policy-makers from all over the world, pointing to a highly active global exchange of conceptual ideas and practical experience.

The debate has raised a number of more fundamental issues relating to the role of policy in economic development. In merging several different policy traditions, cluster policy has drawn attention to the need for a more comprehensive, integrated approach to local economic development and the growing importance of localised policy design and delivery (Nauwelærs, 2001). In requiring a more sophisticated, in-depth understanding of the operation of industrial clusters, it has led to a greater involvement of the private sector in policy-making, highlighting the blurring of boundaries between public and private areas of responsibility in policy (Raines, 2002). Most of all though, the central issue in the debate has been the extent to which the cluster approach represents a new model of understanding and shaping economic development. In tracing the influence of the cluster approach, a wide spectrum of opinion exists, summarised in the following three claims about its impact:

- *cluster as a fad*: the belief that the cluster approach adds little to the existing policy framework and can be discounted as a short-term bandwagon effect;
- *cluster as a catalyst*: where the cluster approach is seen to tweak existing policies and can inspire and channel new developments in policy rather than defining them (a form of 'Trojan horse' effect); and
- *cluster as a paradigm*: the view that the cluster concept has produced a radical and permanent shift in policy interventions in economic development.

'Fad', 'catalyst' and 'paradigm': the following volume aims to discern which of these descriptions best fits the way cluster policies have developed in Europe. It aims to do so by presenting original research on the emergence and operation of cluster policies in the following seven case-study regions, all of which have self-consciously adopted a cluster-based approach to economic development:

- the Arve Valley (France);
- Limburg (the Netherlands);
- North-Rhine Westphalia (Germany);
- País Vasco (Spain);
- Scotland (the UK);
- Styria (Austria); and
- Tampere (Finland).

While all seven regions are pursuing policies targeting industrial clusters, they have been selected with a view to demonstrating the diversity of approaches undertaken within a cluster policy framework. For example, there are differences in terms of the scale of policy, ranging from very large dedicated budgets for cluster development in Scotland and North-Rhine Westphalia (NRW) to far more limited ones in the Arve Valley and Tampere. The regions also vary in terms of their size (e.g. from a population of 60,000 in the Arve Valley to over 17 million in NRW), prosperity and industrial focus of the policy. Moreover, the policies do not necessarily share the same objectives with respect to cluster development. In cases like the País Vasco and Scotland, policy encompasses a wide variety of different aspects of building clusters, while other policies only concentrate on single aspects of cluster development, as in Limburg, where the focus is principally in developing project-based cooperation between firms. The variety should raise questions about the extent to which it is possible to discuss 'cluster policy' as an autonomous area of policy activity. Overall, the various approaches represent individual solutions to common challenges arising from their economic and policy environments.

Six of the case studies are based on research undertaken by the European Policies Research Centre at the University of Strathclyde in the context of the Euro-Cluster project. Funded by several European regional development organisations, the project aimed to identify and understand the key factors behind the successful design and delivery of cluster development policies. Fieldwork consisted of face-to-face interviews with the main policy-making participants in each area and analysis of associated strategies, evaluations and documents. The researchers are grateful to the sponsors for their support.[1] In addition, a seventh case study – Styria – has been added because of the renown of the Styrian cluster approach and its contrasting experiences in pursuing development of two clusters (automobiles and wood products).

The book has been divided into two sections: a review of theory and a report on practice. In the first section, theoretical surveys are provided of the conceptual foundations to cluster development and the existing research understanding of the origins of cluster policy. The second section presents the seven case studies. The chapters broadly have the same internal structure, including a summary of the region's economic structure and main development challenges, the background on the emergence of cluster policy; the design of policy, a description of its content and delivery mechanisms, and lastly, an analysis of its impact on economic development approaches within the region.

Note

[1] The sponsors were: Enterprise Ireland (Ireland); Scottish Enterprise (Scotland, UK); the Scottish Executive (Scotland, UK); the Department of Enterprise, Trade and Industry (Northern Ireland, UK) the Welsh Development Agency (Wales, UK); the Ministry of Local Government and Regional Development (Norway); the East Sweden Development Agency (Östergötland, Sweden); and the Council of Tampere Region (Tampere, Finland).

Part 1: Theory

Chapter 2

Cluster concepts – the social engineering of a new regional institutional fix?

Peter Ache

Introduction

To give an overview of the theoretical debates behind the cluster concept and related models is a quite difficult task, given the duration of the debate and the evolutionary character of the concept itself, not least its derivatives (for an extended treatment see Lagendijk, 1999a). Its history dates back to the beginning of the 1990s, in particular the publication of the seminal book, *The Competitive Advantage of Nations*, by Porter (1990a). From there, the 'cluster' concept very quickly became the object of a wider debate. This debate focused on aspects of competition, innovation, economic and regional restructuring, spatial agglomeration, supply chains, small firm networks, industrial districts and the role of associations (Lagendijk, 1999a, p.18). When examining the advantages of spatial agglomeration, the concept was also linked back to its oldest roots, the work by Alfred Marshall, in particular to his concept of the 'industrial atmosphere' affecting the competitiveness of localised industries (cf. Feser, 1998).

Further, policy-makers, being mainly interested in the application of the concept, developed it further in the course of setting up 'cluster (based or informed) initiatives' for national and later also regional and local economies.[2] There was no single focus or even a single idea anymore. Instead, a flowing concept of different material, procedural and geographical orientations evolved, sometimes tailor-made for very specific national or regional contexts. Even more, looking at the academic actors, different professional backgrounds were involved such as geographers, policy scientists, economists and sociologists. Finally, industry itself has been closely involved in this debate – some of the cases introduced in this book are bottom-up initiatives led by industrialists.

The cluster concept has to be seen as part of a wider debate, which might be called 'new regionalism'. As Lagendijk (1998) critically commented, the new regionalism constitutes a larger agenda comprising concepts such as industrial districts, innovative milieus, regional innovation systems as well as clusters. All of these paradigms have been developed over the past decade (and slightly longer), focusing on one singular though encompassing question: that is, how can innovation in regional industries be stimulated and competitiveness be enhanced and ultimately maintained? In the current chapter, this question will be extended to the wider context, that is, the question of how can a general responsiveness to a rapidly changing environment, often labelled 'globalisation', be achieved?

The chapter will start with the description of Porter's concept and more recent extensions of his ideas. It will then turn towards the processes at work 'inside' clusters. Thereafter, different models of regional industrial organisation will be outlined, which provide an overview on the geographic reach of cluster structures. The last section will outline some conclusions.

Porter's cluster model

Michael Porter's concept of clusters has been the most influential, not least because of its 'applied' and 'prescriptive' character (Lagendijk, 1998). The original cluster concept goes back to *The Competitive Advantage of Nations*.[3] Using a number of case studies from different countries,[4] Porter developed the core concept of the 'diamond of national advantage'. This concept will be introduced first – but only in brief, given the extended literature available, and thereafter, the question of geographical concentration will be addressed. Lastly, the core 'dimensions' of clusters will be outlined.

Porter's main concern was the *competitiveness* of industries or companies and the analysis of its constituent factors. When examining the foundations of national competitiveness, Porter (1990b, p.77) argued: "The answer lies in four broad attributes of a nation, attributes that individually and as a system constitute the diamond of national advantage, the playing field that each nation establishes and operates for its industries." The attributes are (cf. Figure 2.1):

- *factor conditions*: the nation's position in factors of production, such as skilled labour or infrastructure, necessary to compete in a given industry;
- *demand conditions*: the nature of home-market demand for the industry's product or service;

8

- *related and supporting industries*: the presence or absence in the nation of supplier industries and other related industries that are internationally competitive; and
- *firm strategy, structure and rivalry*: the conditions in the nation governing how companies are created, organised and managed, as well as the nature of domestic rivalry.

As Porter (1990b, p.77) explained:

Each point on the diamond – and the diamond as a system – affects essential ingredients for achieving international competitive success: the availability of resources and skills necessary for competitive advantage in an industry; the information that shapes the opportunities that companies perceive and the directions in which they deploy their resources and skills; the goals of the owners, managers, and individuals in companies; and most important, the pressures on companies to invest and innovate.

Figure 2.1: The diamond of national advantage

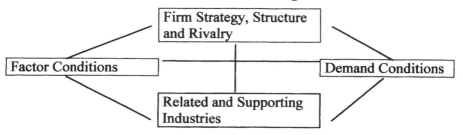

Source: Porter, 1990b.

In addition, the diamond has a clear *systemic character*, which means that individual factors cannot be considered in isolation from each other. Porter makes this clear in his recommendations on what can be done by governments and companies in turn. On the contrary, it would be a misunderstanding of his model if actors simply try to provide factors in all these areas and in exactly the same way. Porter points out that in the current global competition, which includes amongst other things the possibility for companies to relocate productive activities on a global scale, it is rather a search for 'differential advantages', that is highly specific factor conditions and support structures, which have to be developed (see also Enright, 2000 on this aspect).

The differential advantages are a point of entry for local and regional circumstances or environmental conditions. As the title of Porter's book indicates, the concept in its original form focused on the *national level*, on states competing in a global market, and on firms or specific industries. The *regional dimension* (and the dimension of the city, Porter, 1995) was only established later on, and mainly in a debate led by geographers and regional economists.

Porter spoke about 'geographical concentration' while developing arguments for *dynamic improvements*, spurred by domestic rivalry (Porter 1990b, p.82):

> Domestic rivalry... creates pressure on companies to innovate and improve. Local rivals push each other to lower costs, improve quality and service, and create new products and processes. But unlike rivalries with foreign competitors ... local rivalries often go beyond pure economic or business competition and become intensely personal... Geographical concentration magnifies the power of domestic rivalry.

The term *domestic* (and local) has no immediate geographical connotation at the outset, at least in the sense of a *defined* region. The regional geographic dimension, with the region usually understood as a smaller distinctive part of the national territory, comes as an addition. Porter provided the example of highly specialised industrial districts based on cutlery companies in Solingen (West Germany) and Seki (Japan).

Today, the geographic aspect has become more important in the debate, even in Porter's own writings. The importance of all the elements of local production systems interacting with each other can be seen in recent Porter comments, quoted by Asheim (1999a, p.14), where he defined clusters as "geographic concentrations of interconnected companies and institutions in a particular field... encompass(ing) an array of linked industries and other specialised inputs such as components, machinery, and services, and providers of specialised infrastructure." He further noted that clusters not only have vertical value chain links, but can extend 'laterally' to manufacturers in sectors similar by dint of related products, technologies, skills or inputs. Cluster not only consist of businesses, but a range of other organisations including research institutes, training providers and governmental bodies.

This provides a first insight into the material side of clusters as well as some of the 'procedural' dimensions, or the *glue* which keeps the cluster together. On the basis of Enright (2000), these material elements can be classified according to the following series of different criteria.[5] Combining these different criteria demonstrates the diversity of potential and actual clusters which can exist in a regional economy:

- *geographic scope:* the territorial extent of the firms, customers, suppliers, support services and institutions forming the cluster (in some cases, they can actually be non-existent, as with 'virtual' clusters, which are based on geographically-extended ICT networks);
- *density:* the sheer number and economic weight of companies in clusters, ranging from 'dense' to 'sparse';
- *breadth:* the range of horizontally-related industries (e.g. sharing a common technology, supplying the same end-users, using the same distribution channels) – again in terms of features, these can be 'narrow' (with only a few industries and supply chains) or 'broad' (with a variety of products in closely related industries);
- *depth:* the range of vertically-related industries, which constitute the cluster – from 'deep' (complete or nearly complete supply chains) to 'shallow' (inputs, components, equipment, technology and support services come from outside);
- *activity base:* the number and nature of the activities in the value-added chain that are performed, varying between 'activity rich' (where most critical activities are performed locally – core strategy-setting, product or service development, marketing and corporate coordination) and 'activity poor' (basically the absence of the previous list);
- *growth potential:* the demand for the product or the service provided by the cluster, varying from young, innovative products to mature, outdated products – similarly, depending on the product cycle, the competitive position can differ (labelled as 'sunrise', 'noonday' or 'sunset', and 'competitive' or 'non-competitive');
- *innovative capacity:* here, it is not a question of 'high' or 'low' tech but rather a question of high innovation or low innovation *activity*;
- *industrial organisation:* the relationships among firms in the cluster in terms of the nature of relationship and the distribution of power; and
- *coordination:* the coordination mechanisms and inter-firm relations, varying between hierarchies, markets or intermediate forms.

Finally, Enright (2000, p.322f.) identified different states of cluster development, which he termed: working clusters, latent clusters, potential clusters, and 'wishful thinking' clusters.

Working clusters are those clusters "in which a critical mass of local knowledge, expertise, personnel, and resources create agglomeration economies that are used by firms to their advantage in competing with those outside the cluster." In such clusters we find dense and complex patterns of competition and cooperation among local firms and are able to attract mobile resources and key personnel from other locations.

Latent clusters "have a critical mass of firms in related industries sufficient to reap the benefits of clustering, but have not developed the level of interaction and information flows necessary to truly benefit from co-location." This can be due to a lack of knowledge of other local firms, of interaction among firms and individuals, of a shared vision of their future, or of the requisite level of trust for firms to find and exploit common interests.

Potential clusters "are those that have some of the elements necessary for the development of successful clusters, but where these elements must be deepened and broadened in order to benefit from the impact of agglomeration." Often there are important gaps in the inputs, services or information flows that support cluster development. Like latent clusters, they lack the interaction and self awareness of working clusters.

'Wishful thinking' clusters are "those chosen by governments for support, but which lack a critical mass of firms or favourable conditions for organic development." Many of the electronics and biotechnology 'clusters' found in government programmes fall into this category. Other wishful thinking clusters are those such as 'manufacturing' or 'high technology' that are far too broad to act meaningfully as clusters.

Procedural dimensions – the example of the local innovative milieu

The preceding sections introduced a number of elements which are considered to be important in the internal organisation of clusters and the effects which they have on participating companies. However, the question is, what makes the sector-based grouping more than just the sum of its constituent parts?

As mentioned at the outset, an overarching concept that captures the entirety could be labelled 'response capacity'. In a basic sense, the response capacity points to the capabilities of companies to respond to changes in the market environment. From the range of new regionalism paradigms available, the example of the 'local innovative milieu' focuses on this response capacity in particular (Ache, 2000). It also states that it is in fact the region which creates innovative companies – i.e. companies which have a relatively high response capacity.

Whereas the original cluster approach by Porter considered the elements of the diamond mainly without a specific geographical or regional view and whereas the cluster model is also weak regarding societal aspects, the local innovative milieu focuses in particular on the conditions of regional societies which enhance the response capacity. The growing awareness of the importance of regional factors and environments in economic development is partly due to the fact that a small number of specific regions have been discussed time and again as outstandingly successful in terms of innovation performance and global competitiveness.[6] These regions have been analysed on the one hand in terms of how advanced modern industries shape the region, and on the other, how regions in turn influence the development prospects and the structure of advanced industries. This awareness also partly derives from the re-detection of 'socio-economics', that is the importance of the social regulation models existing for an economy in regions (Amin and Thrift, 1995).

The model of the 'local innovative milieu' has been developed from an innovation perspective. Increasing the innovative performance in rapidly changing market environments is considered to be its most important task. The main target group is usually SMEs (or even so-called 'ultra small' businesses). However, industrial innovation is only one aspect of the issue: as will be shown later, other aspects regarding the response capacity of the regional society have to be considered as well.

The paradigm of the local innovative milieu was first introduced about 15 years ago by GREMI (*Groupe de Recherche Europeen sur les Milieux Innovateurs*). Their central hypothesis states that the existence of companies is not to be seen as separate from their surrounding milieu but rather as a product of it. A local innovative milieu can be considered as an incubator of innovations and innovative companies within a given territory. Innovative conduct will also be imprinted on by local, regional and national influences. In the words of Aydalot and Keeble (1988, p.9, emphasis added): "This line of argument leads naturally to the hypothesis *that it is often the local environment which is, in effect, the entrepreneur and innovator*, rather than the firm."

Camagni (1991b, p.2) draws our attention to aspects of co-location, synergy, personal relations and networks which are also important: "All these elements in fact are crucial... not only because they widely determine the efficiency of the local production system, but particularly because they determine the local response capability to a changing external environment, its innovativeness and production flexibility." This regional capacity to respond is a very important feature of the milieu and is emphasised when looking at the constituent parts of a local innovative milieu. The milieu cannot be taken as merely another 'warehouse', offering a toolkit for innovation which a company or actor resorts to at will. Instead, the basic elements of the milieu can be found in organisational and functional terms as defined by Maillat (1991, p.113):

- "a collection of players": each of these players (whether businesses, universities, government agencies or otherwise) should have relative[7] autonomy with respect to strategic decision-making;
- "physical elements (firms, infrastructure) but also non-physical elements (know-how) and institutional elements";
- "an interaction logic which forms part of cooperation": in other words, the milieu's key actors should act 'interdependently' to maximise usage of existing resources; and
- "a learning logic", as demonstrated by the capacity of actors to adapt their actions in response to changes in their economic environment.

Overall, the local innovative milieu concept presents itself as a complex local system with economically, socially and technologically interdependent processes prominent. In other words, it can be described as a coherent territorial production system. Notions of coherence and process are important here. Processes of communication, frequent interaction and learning form a local culture in the longer term with local actors (i.e. companies, individuals and organisations) developing a shared world view, labelled as a *common approach to situations, problems, opportunities* or a *coherent system of representations* (Crevoisier, (1990); see also for a more recent but not GREMI-related discussion, Asheim, (1999a)).

The paradigm of the local innovative milieu has been criticised as being rather abstract and vague, not least within GREMI itself (Lagendijk, 1996; Storper, 1995). GREMI provided adjustments to the basic concept and attempted to enhance its clarity. The new dimensions utilised for this purpose come from evolutionary economics (as developed by Nelson and Winter, 1982), network behaviour of firms (e.g. Bergman, Maier and Tödtling, 1991; Camagni, 1991a) and the respective spatial focus of these concepts.

In this revised 'hard' form of the local innovative milieu, networks contribute to the working of the milieu and, from an evolutionary perspective, functions designed to cope with uncertainty are introduced. The latter function is labelled as the search-selection-signalling-transcoding-transformer-control – or SSSTTC – function, the core concept of the 'response capacity' mentioned at the beginning of this section.

The SSSTTC function defines the relationship between the milieu and its environment – and here we can find central features of the 'region'.

- *Search function.* The milieu is a collective information broker, continually scrutinising the environment (e.g. technology monitoring) and providing structured information.
- *Selection function.* Decision-making routines and firm-specific management styles form the basis of this function.
- *Signalling function.* The milieu acts as a 'lighthouse' signalling developments or needs to the outside world, but also internally creating awareness.
- *Transcoding function.* Information available in the wider environment is translated into codes which are comprehensible for local companies: transcoding activities turn unorganised information flows into a company-specific 'knowledge' which can be used to enhance business activities. In this way, the milieu is learning from the outside environment and translating external developments according to the needs of the milieu.
- *Transformer function.* The milieu helps to internalise external energies or resources and establishes structures to reduce complexity (e.g. organisational structures).
- *Control function.* The milieu collectively defines and coordinates management styles and decision routines.

· These functions will be performed by local actors and institutions and can partly or explicitly be taken on by public organisations such as universities. Altogether, these functions also describe the 'glue' which keeps a cluster together.

Clusters as sticky places in space – new industrial districts

The following section will turn away from processes internal to the cluster and instead focus on the spatial form. The main core of any cluster is its companies, though typically it includes other economic agents such as training providers, research institutes, public sector agencies, etc. The internal and external organisational structures which these companies take provide further criteria for analysing clusters or providing a cluster typology. An interesting approach to this has been made by Anne

Markusen (1996) who devised four different cluster models: the Marshallian industrial district (henceforth MID; Markusen worked with the modern Italianate variant); hub-and-spoke districts; satellite industrial platforms; and state-centred districts.

Markusen started from the Italianate variant of the MID and rigorously applied the concept to the US situation to find out the degree to which the concept might be found outside of Italy. This, in principle, was questioning the transferability of the model to different circumstances. Her findings show that a number of models can be defined and that there is not just a single form.

The *Marshallian industrial district* consists of many small enterprises which make investment and production decisions locally. Outside linkages are minimal. As Markusen explained (1996, p.299):

> What makes the industrial district so special and vibrant, in Marshall's account, is the nature and quality of the local labour market, which is internal to the district and highly flexible. Individuals move from firm to firm, and owners as well as workers live in the same community, where they benefit from the fact that 'the secrets of industry are in the air'.

This cultural aspect can in particular be found at the basis of the modern Italianate version of the MID, which have generated 'resilient cultures' through deep-rooted socio-political traditions and communal continuity. Markusen found such districts to be characterised by governance bodies able to take on leadership roles and a strong degree of coordination between key economic participants (such as unions and businesses) ensuring relative income stability.

The *hub-and-spoke model* of the industrial district is a region with one or more companies and/or central facilities as a core around which supplier and related activities spread like the spokes of a wheel. An example of this can be seen with Boeing in Seattle. The dynamics of this district are defined – if not dominated – by the main nodal company/facility, though over time, the structure of companies, suppliers and services might diversify and change more towards agglomeration economies.

Satellite platform industrial districts are congregations of branch facilities of externally-based multi-plant firms. Markusen characterised these as often being "a way of stimulating regional development in outlying areas." The companies or facilities have to have a 'stand alone' character, which means they are independent from the direct environment. As Markusen (1996, p.304) further said: "Its most conspicuous feature is the absence of any connections or networks within the region and the predominance of links to the parent corporation and other branch plants elsewhere." Examples of this are routine assembly lines as well as the RTD parts of companies. The dynamics of this cluster are mainly controlled from the outside, with a permanent threat of relocating the plants due to their medium-term mobility.

The last model is *state-anchored districts*, based on public or non-profit organisations around which other firms and organisations clusters. Examples of this are a military base or a university where the local economic structure can be dominated by these entities. The effect of universities in their regions has received much interest in the recent past (cf. CURDS, 2000).

Conclusions

In the previous sections, the chapter has outlined the basics of the cluster concept, in terms of the underlying theoretical debates, structures and processes. Despite the various attempts to define clusters, the concept still shows a considerable degree of variance, as will also be seen from the case studies. Furthermore, given the variety of actors involved, clusters can have a range of different meanings; in a sense, it is open to a variety of strategic interpretations.

When looking at clusters, we have to differentiate between material and procedural characteristics. Furthermore, clusters have to be distinguished regarding their geographical reach (especially concentrated regional clusters).[8] Different policy options are linked to the different levels under consideration (which explains to a degree Porter's critical view on 'national' policies, whereas on the contrary, on a regional level, a number of policies to support clusters can be devised).

Regarding the material aspects, in a nutshell, clusters might be defined as industries or companies with formal input-output or buyer-supplier linkages, which are geographically co-located, which share business-related local institutions, and show evidence of informal cooperative competition. Beyond that, the processes at work inside the cluster might be captured with the response capacity, discussed in the case of the milieu as being based e.g. on the search-selection-signalling-transcoding-transformer-control function. These different functions constitute a dense locational interaction which has a considerable influence beyond the purely economic sphere, incorporating the local civil society. This strong degree of 'embeddedness' is on the one hand seen to form the competitive edge of successful regions. The challenge in a global economy, with accelerated business cycles and intensified competition, is to develop a comprehensive regional response capacity. This capacity is not only provided by companies and firms as the main economic actors but also by other non-economic actors from local, regional and national levels.

The chapter title – the social engineering of a new regional institutional fix – deliberately points to the ambivalence behind the cluster concept and strategies. It links the cluster debate back to some more analytical aspects, derived from a discussion of the relation between structures and agency (Ache, 2000) as well as the role of new institutions, in particular within technology policy (Kitschelt, 1996, Nauwelaers, 2001).

A previous paragraph pointed to globalisation as one of the challenges for which a cluster strategy provides a response. The globalisation paradigm itself is very ambivalent, especially regarding the effects of this process (cf. Held and McGrew, 2000). When looking at concrete examples of regional cluster projects, which always come with a reference to the globalisation challenge, the question can be raised, whether the cluster approach is rather more interested in certain institutional and societal changes than economic success factors? As one of the later examples will show for the situation in Germany, the cluster policy can help to establish a new social regulation mode[9] in a hitherto fairly stable environment (see also Lovering, 1999). This can be seen as a positive event, breaking up petrified structures and giving way to innovation; but, this might also be seen as negative, destroying existing social institutions. Similarly, the fuzziness of the cluster concept (in both respects, material and ideological) requires the establishment of wide coalitions amongst stakeholders.[10] Both, clusters but also milieus, can be seen as building bridges between different elements of a societal space[11] – again, very often bypassing traditional institutional structures. This can include also a more 'symbolic' element, as the case studies elaborate with respect to the sense of identity exhibited by clusters.

The bridging function is relevant for the purely technological or innovation aspect, too. The cluster is considered to be the adequate response in times, where the technological process can be characterised as increasingly 'complex and interactive' with 'loose causal connections' (Kitschelt, 1996). These features call for hybrid institutions at the border between public and private realms, based on voluntary associations.[12] Having said this, one important aspect continues to stay uncertain, that is which of the organisational forms is the most efficient, with a view to the longitude and uncertainty of future development rounds? Despite all high hopes, overall the technological growth model is rather one of jobless growth (Lovering, 1999). A negative sum game between a few winning and many losing locations is very likely. A race for a permanently decreasing global share has been created and leads to a waste of resources spend by a majority of losers in that process. On the positive side, political and local actors, being aware about their resource scarcity try to apply a thorough understanding of the cluster concept to avoid wasting resources further.

In the end, in analogy with the 'old' regulationist' analysis of technology impacts as depending on the wider regulation model, the cluster concept, its obvious variations and finally also its results have to be understood as contingent and dependant (cf. Boyer, 1988). The national and regional context is decisive in the application of cluster policies – and we cannot expect the same institutional fix for all regions. However, the arena for the social engineering approach continues to be the 'region'. If globalisation can be understood as a process creating various re-territorialisations (cf. Brenner, 1999) with the emergence of polycentric urban regions as the main feature, the question is, how do we create on that regional level a response capacity matching the globalisation challenge?

Notes

[2] Partly also provided for by Porter himself, as his recent writings suggest, e.g. his comments on the competitive advantage of the city, thereby narrowing down his previously national concept to a smaller geographical scale (Porter, 1995).

[3] In the current paper we use as the main reference, Porter (1990b), which provides a good overview on the book and is recommended here for any reader short in time. The book itself extends the argument and especially elaborates on the national case studies.

[4] A four-year study of ten important trading nations – Denmark, Germany, Italy, Japan, Korea, Singapore, Sweden, Switzerland, the UK and the US – was conducted by Porter's research team. The applied methodology mainly consisted of an identification of internationally successful industries (using available statistical data and field interviews).

[5] Another set of cluster 'dimensions' can be found in Lagendijk (1999a).

[6] Like the Third Italy (with Emilia-Romagna as core region), Baden-Württemberg (Germany), Jutland (Denmark), M-4 Corridor (UK) etc.

[7] This 'relative' independence has to be understood in terms of the 'critical functions', mentioned by Enright (2000): core strategy-setting, product or service development, marketing and corporate coordination functions.

[8] Other examples can be 'virtual' or 'global' clusters. For the Dutch case, 'mega clusters' have been defined as a subdivision of a national economy. Jacobs (1997) provides as examples: assembling industries, chemical industries, energy, agro-food, construction, media, health, and commercial and non-commercial services, which have been defined using input-output analysis.

[9] The introduction of labour pools of precarious jobs which goes along with an increased uncertainty on the side of organised labour.

[10] Facilitated by a EU system of mainly 'negotiated' capitalist states (Dunford and Benko, 1991).

[11] This is a reference to the paradigm of the so-called matrix-space, see Ache (2000). The elements are that of substrata (e.g. industries), action (e.g. politicians) and regulation (e.g. administrations).

[12] Amin and Thrift (1995) have addressed this topic also, but with an emphasis on civil society.

Chapter 3

Cluster policy – does it exist?

Philip Raines

Introduction

After a decade of academic and policy-making debate surrounding cluster development theory and practice – accelerated if not necessarily launched by Michael Porter's work – the terms of inquiry have begun to shift. With respect to cluster policy – that set of public sector interventions designed to influence cluster development – attention is moving away from simple reporting and description of cluster policy activity to more intensive investigations, if not challenges, about its substance. The existence of cluster policy is not in itself controversial – over the last decade, there has been a global proliferation of self-styled 'cluster' policies. The terminology of cluster development has informed economic, sectoral and spatial development policies at national, regional and local levels. The use of the analytical tools associated with cluster policy is not only widespread in Western Europe and North America (Roelandt and den Hertog, 1999), but increasingly in less-developed parts of the world as well (Schmitz and Nadvi, 1999). As a coherent policy approach, it has been promoted by international development organisations, such as the European Commission, OECD and UNIDO, and led to the formation of policy-maker associations interested in pursuing cluster development, such as the Competitiveness Institute.

Moreover, most cluster policies seem to show some coherence by self-consciously drawing on the same theoretical sources. Again, the pervasive influence of Porter's ideas has been critical, not just through his published work and the business consultancy with which he is associated (Monitor), but also a host of policy-making conferences explicitly engaging with the Porter conceptual framework. As will be seen through the case studies in this volume, the concepts underpinning policy and the policies themselves have been in a constant and reiterative process of mutual re-definition. Nevertheless, the vocabulary and many of the theoretical tools used share common origins, even if they have resulted in quite varied outcomes. While no one can quite pinpoint what it is, 'cluster policy' is increasingly regarded as a policy area as substantive as, say, 'foreign investment policy' or (more relevantly) 'innovation policy'.

Nevertheless, questions have been consistently raised about whether the cluster concept has simply 'hijacked' economic development policy discourse by re-labelling existing policy approaches with little added value, or 'piggy-backed' it by extending the existing policy concepts through the introduction of novel frameworks, targets, instruments and processes of policy intervention. Put simply, to what extent can 'cluster policy' be said to exist as an autonomous, distinctive area of public sector endeavour? Indeed, how does the cluster concept (or the range of contested concepts) map onto the current portfolio of policy approaches to influencing economic development? As a means of providing context for the case studies, the following chapter explores these issues by reviewing the background to the current enthusiasm for cluster development by policy-makers: first, by discussing the definitional problems arising from the diversity of policies claiming to shape cluster development; and subsequently, by considering the relationship between what are currently termed 'cluster policies' and their antecedent policy traditions.

Defining 'cluster policy'

Debate about what constitutes cluster policy raises questions about the extent to which any set of policy interventions can be said to have a common, let alone standardised content. For example, arguments have long run over the theoretical and practical limits and composition of regional/spatial development policy (for a review, see Bachtler, 2000). However, if cluster policy is not unique in this regard, there is a more acute problem with cluster policy because of its historical roots in – and continuing overlap with – other policy areas and the wide diversity in the content of cluster policies. Despite common conceptual starting points and shared language, its definition remains a thorny task.

To say cluster policy is simply 'policy to develop clusters' only shunts the definitional problem back to the issue of what constitutes a cluster. The previous chapter outlined the multiplicity of theoretical responses to the issues of industrial competitiveness and agglomeration highlighted by, and intersecting in, the work of Porter. The fuzziness of the target of cluster policies is reflected in the portfolio of working definitions used for a 'cluster', ranging from simple commercial networks to traditional sectors to more sophisticated inter-sectoral, business-academic groupings. Moreover, a cynical (and to an extent, justifiably so) suggestion has often been made that cluster policies can often be mislabelled networking policies, consisting of little more than uncoordinated bundles of existing policies of industry assistance and innovation support under a new family name. Despite the apparent injunction of cluster development literature for a conceptual paradigm to underlie policy, any cursory review of cluster policies demonstrates that the active paradigms of policy-makers are frequently both ill-defined and highly contested.

The problem of definition is further compounded by the patchy theoretical support for policy intervention in cluster development by many of its 'ur-texts'. The major cluster theory models either do not place much emphasis on policy or have described its role in generalised terms. For example, Porter (1990a) – at least in his original development of the cluster model – argued that policy intervention had little role in the emergence of clusters. Policy should be restricted to creating the environment in which clusters emerged, an 'indirect' rather than a direct role. While his later writings suggest greater scope for policy intervention in developing the 'public goods' supporting clusters (see, for example, Porter, 1998), Porter remains wary of industrial targeting by governments in cluster development, echoing the extensive distrust to 'picking winners' in industry which permeates government policy in the developed world. In addition, some have openly speculated on the value of the Porterian analysis in guiding policy-makers in cluster development in the first place (see, for example, Davies and Ellis, 2000).

The 'innovative milieu' concept – one of the main parallel 'cluster' frameworks to the Porter model – partially foresees a greater role for policy, though the issue has not been systematically investigated in GREMI studies. Maillat (1996) noted that as the local productive system is constantly dynamic, the scope existed for 'territorial policy' to influence the factors which contributed to the emergence of an innovative milieu. In arguing that the role of such policy is "to strengthen the symbiosis between the different elements in the local productive system in order to ensure its flexibility and its integration in the global economy" (Maillat, 1996, p.77), policy can strengthen the points in the innovative milieu where these elements are weak. Camagni (1995) argued that such policy interventions need to be constantly adapted to reinforce the local environment (especially in terms of infrastructure and human resources) and to encourage network linkages between milieu participants. There are specific functions which policy can take on in the SSSTTC model outlined in the previous chapter – as, for example, with respect to 'search' (policy as an information broker) and 'signalling' (policy as a technology monitor) functions. Nevertheless, while acknowledging the theoretical role of policy, the GREMI school writings provide few pointers for its practical manifestations.

More emphasis again has been placed on the role of public institutions in the 'learning region' writings of Cooke and Morgan (1998), Florida (1995) *et al*. Here, institutions can act as 'animateurs' of local innovation systems, not only identifying the points in the regional economy where self-sustaining innovation can be activated, but also becoming major actors in promoting the creation of networks. Indeed, it is particularly *regional* institutions that are regarded as having a strong policy rationale. While stopping long short of advocating an industrial policy that subsidises particular sectors, the approach acknowledges the need to direct scarce public resources towards supporting certain parts of the economy. It does not though purport to provide a policy framework for *cluster* development, only a system in which a region's overall innovation capacity can be enhanced (an important but arguably not sufficient element in cluster policy).

The ambivalence about the role of the public sector demonstrated in writings about the cluster concept is further reflected in direct commentaries on cluster policy. Research has uncovered quite different approaches to cluster development. For example, in a survey of practice in OECD countries, Boekholt and Thuriaux (1999) distinguished between four separate models of cluster policy: the 'national advantage' model, in which policy is targeted at national-level clusters; the 'SME networking' model, concentrating on localised, typically indigenous SME networks; the 'regional cluster development' model, in which a wide array of policy tools are used to support broadly-based cluster groups; and a 'research-industry relations' model, where policy is more narrowly focused on business-university RTD linkages. While the four models are not mutually incompatible, the goals and priorities for actions implicit in each are often quite separate. Similarly, reviewing European policy support for cluster-based innovation, Nauwelærs laid out a long list of different forms of cluster policy, noting that the policy did not so much exist as a self-contained, and therefore more easily defined field of activity, but as an "innovative combination of existing policy instruments from traditional policy fields" (Nauwelærs, 2001, p.100).

Despite the hazy boundaries of cluster policy, it is possible to identify common features in their design and implementation which separate them from parallel and preceding policy areas (see, for example, Benneworth and Charles, 2001). These core concepts derive from a series of often locally-specific dialogues between the new insights into economic and industrial development provided by cluster development literature and existing policy frameworks. While the results may differ, they tend to be shaped around the same set of shared policy issues. These can be grouped under three areas: the importance of networking; the targeting of selected networks; and the focus on innovation (Raines, 2001a).

First, cluster policies concentrate their support in networks rather than individual firms. These networks are not regarded automatically as traditional sectoral groupings, but are frequently defined in terms of inter-sectoral value chains which link large firms, SMEs, research providers and public sector institutions together. The policy goal has been to facilitate the development of the network rather than promote the growth of its constituent agents. Consequently, public sector interventions aim to improve growth conditions for the cluster as a whole and are not restricted to subsidising the activities of particular firms within the cluster. Measures provide common resources for groups of inter-related organisations – such as specialised infrastructure or export marketing/branding programmes – or encourage linkages between and amongst firms and universities (CEC, 1999a). In this, cluster policy has been presented as a natural evolution of Lagendijk's concept of regional policy targeting the relationships between a region's 'relational assets' (whether such assets are concentrated in specific institutions, as, for example, a prominent firm or university, or diffused throughout the economy, as with a set of skills) rather than the assets *per se* (Lagendijk, 1999b).

Second, following on from this point, cluster policy is generally concerned with only *selected* networks. The approach enables the concentration of policy resources in the parts of the region's industrial structure which are likely to show the greatest benefit, a form of 'picking winners', but one that is perhaps more sophisticated than the traditional industrial policy goal of supporting indigenous champions. Where a local development strategy has been steeped in the cluster concept, this has implications for the implicit model of regional economic growth being advocated. Rather than addressing the systemic needs of the local economy as a whole, policy is preferentially favouring the development of a handful of sectors. By boosting the competitiveness of these sectors, a form of 'growth pole' approach is effectively being promoted, recalling the ideas of Perroux (1950) and the growth-centre development policies of the 1960s and 1970s, but with a greater sensitivity to the framework conditions for in which these growth centres (now re-termed 'clusters') form (see Feser, 1998, for a discussion). The aim – whether explicit or not – seems to be for these sectoral value chains to become the spines around which wider economic development can take place through a series of multiplier effects in income, employment and research and productivity performance.

This is also reflected in the high degree of private sector participation in the design and delivery of cluster policy, unusually so when compared with related policy areas (such as traditional industrial policy) (Raines, 2002). Indeed, some commentators have argued that this interactive quality in policy-making is the distinguishing characteristic of cluster policy (Nauwelærs, 2001). Although cluster policies have largely been public sector-initiated, they feature strong involvement from the private sector. This has directly resulted from the requirements of the public sector in developing a cluster policy, especially with respect to the gathering of policy intelligence about the cluster. Given the importance in cluster policy of being able to target specific gaps in the value chain or business environment hindering cluster development, substantial consultation with private sector agents in the outlines of policy has necessarily been widespread and unusually intensive. Cluster policy often involves significant participation with the cluster agents themselves in delivering the policy, principally through their contributions to the strategic direction and targets of the cluster policy in the initial strategy-making phase, their joint financing of cluster-based projects and assistance in policy implementation (for example, through private sector intermediaries contracted to delivery parts of the cluster policy). In a sense, the policy aims to enable the main actors in a cluster to take responsibility for maintaining its competitiveness over time. A good example of this is high degree of private sector participation in País Vasco cluster policy, as detailed in a later chapter.

The third defining feature of cluster policies is that they prioritise the goal of enhancing innovation and learning within the cluster. In this respect, the policies overlap extensively with more 'traditional' innovation support policy areas. What is perhaps new in the policy is the targeting on particular sectors rather than the innovation system of a region in its entirety (as argued in some national/regional innovation system literature), operating on the implicit principle that innovation is a function of specific networks which are a subset of the innovation system as a whole. Indeed, within such policies, clusters can be defined as networks which are bound and delimited by intensive and repeated knowledge transactions occurring far more often than in other parts of the economy, thereby requiring fewer policy resources to generate step-level changes in industrial competitiveness.

Multi-dimensional support for innovation has been widely recognised as central to cluster-based policies (Lagendijk, 1999b; Roelandt and den Hertog, 1999). Although differing in specifics, rationales for cluster policies have usually focused on the common issues of the production of knowledge, the importance of learning and the use of both in the local economy (Asheim, 1999b). In large part, this is a recognition of two important insights into economic development which have been popularised in recent years. First, it demonstrates a greater awareness of the role of knowledge and innovation in sustaining the competitive advantage of sectors and, more importantly, the structures in place to ensure that such knowledge can be generated on an on-going basis, diffused throughout a particular sector/region and transformed into products and services which will enhance individual businesses' competitiveness (Temple, 1998). Innovation is no longer seen as a linear process, but part of a complex series of interactions between different functions within a company (such as marketing, human resource management, etc). Further, there has not only been a renewed interest in the sources of innovation – with increased attention on innovation occurring *between* businesses (and other organisations) rather than simply *within* them – but its transfer within (and between) sectors and regions.

This proceeds from an understanding that such knowledge and innovation are *localised* processes, made possible by the geographical proximity of a range of interlinked institutions (including businesses, universities and policy organisations) (Storper, 1997). Proximity and innovation have been closely linked through a renewed understanding of the role of trust and cooperation in the development of collective learning. Innovation is perceived to be the function of a local *system* of businesses, research institutes and other agents rather than the output of isolated firms. Policy-makers have increasingly realised that such systems are more likely to occur in a regional group of firms and other institutions which have achieved a certain critical mass, where linkages can be denser and stronger and the local environment/milieu can underpin these networks.

The commonalities of cluster policy also extend to their modes of influence. Although cluster policies can vary significantly in content, as with any field of policy activity, they typically focus on the same types of market failure. As a result, policy interventions can be grouped in terms of how they target the points in the development of a cluster where markets alone cannot always generate the necessary elements. These can be viewed in the stylised model of a cluster in Figure 3.1: while the model cannot claim to represent the cluster concept lying behind all cluster policies, it can be used to display the three main points at which policy seeks to affect clusters: through the interactions within the cluster itself; through commonly-accessed factors influencing the competitiveness of the cluster as a whole; and in terms of the cluster's self-awareness.

Figure 3.1: Key features in cluster dynamics

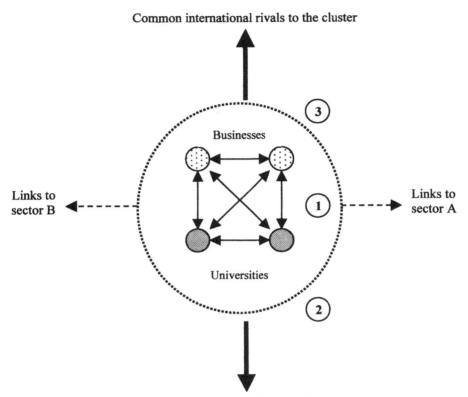

First, and ultimately, clusters are defined by the interactions amongst their main agents, frequently inter-sectoral and involving both businesses and research providers such as universities (as shown in **1** in the figure above). To develop networking among potential cluster participants, policy must create the conditions for cooperation as well as increase – or at least, highlight – the incentives to take part. Various policy measures support this activity, including: measures to increase the incentives for cooperation on RTD and technology transfer; targeted inward investment to attract new agents into the cluster; the provision of publicly-funded infrastructure such as science parks to encourage interactive agglomerations; and the public sector acting as brokers for cluster agents interested in finding partners. All of these have been recurring tools of intervention in cluster policies.

Second, central to a cluster is the presence of common competitive advantages which are external to individual firms but internal to the cluster as a whole (as shown by **2**). When Alfred Marshall wrote about industrial districts, he pointed to common labour markets of specialised skills as one such advantage for firms operating in the same economic sphere and geographical area, but advantages can include special research excellence (in a firm or a university) and other forms of tacit knowledge that are specific to the region. Many cluster policies aim to increase that tacit knowledge through a series of measures focusing on developing these common competitive advantages. For the most part, they are pitched at developing common resources which will improve the competitiveness of a group of firms within the cluster, such as access to key business information, technological and business infrastructure, technology transfer, tailored skills training and venture capital provision.

Lastly, cluster identity can be the subject of cluster policy. While the cluster's collective awareness of itself – usually defined with reference to external rivals (**3** in Figure 3.1) – is not necessarily critical for cluster development, it has been a persistent feature of cluster policy. This can take the form of 'identity building': defining the limits of the cluster in the first place; supporting the initial association of the cluster; and increasing members' understanding of the cluster and their sense of 'belonging' to it. It can also involve 'identity projecting' by defining an image of the cluster which can be used in collective marketing exercises. The measures involved in this include cluster mapping exercises, external promotion and marketing of the cluster, setting up cluster representative organisations and providing information on technology and market trends through foresight studies and benchmarking with the cluster's main competitors.

Tracing the roots of cluster policy

Just as cluster policy represents the confluence of different conceptual traditions intersecting in Porter's work (as discussed in the previous chapter), it is also the results of distinct *policy* streams interacting. In the debate over the emergence of cluster policy, the focus has been on the additional elements the policy brings to its predecessors or at least the way in which existing policies have been reconfigured within a new conceptual framework – no one has challenged the considerable debt of current cluster policy to previous policy traditions (Enright, 2000; Feser, 1998). Indeed, the definition of cluster policy is largely set by its ability to re-combine related but hitherto autonomous policy traditions (Mariussen, 2001). As

Boekholt and Thuriaux (1999, p.384) noted: "Cluster policies are situated at the boundaries of industrial policy (including SME policy), regional development policy, and science and technology policy." To trace this process, it is worthwhile examining how each of these policy areas have fed into cluster policy.

The close links between cluster and industrial policy are visible in the extensive use of the cluster approach in national industrial policies, for example, in the UK with respect to biotechnology (Shohet, 1998) and industrial policy in general in both Denmark (Drejer *et al*, 1999) and the Netherlands (Roelandt *et al*, 1999). As Porter (1998) has argued, cluster policy differs significantly from 'traditional' industrial policy:

- it does not concentrate simply on fostering emerging, high-tech or restructuring declining, mature industries (though these sectors do feature strongly in many cluster policies), but can be applied to a range of industrial sectors exhibiting international competitiveness;
- it does not exclusively target individual firms, but business networks, often with a more pronounced emphasis on SMEs, a point also made by Boekholt and Thuriaux (1999); and
- its measures do not aim to subsidise, but to provide more indirect, facilitative forms of intervention.

However, in the decade prior to the rapid emergence of cluster policy, industrial and sectoral policy had been showing what might be regarded as strong 'cluster' tendencies. New approaches to industrial policy in the 1980s dovetailed neatly with the insights of the cluster approach. Industrial policy had already gravitated towards more systemic public sector interventions, as most apparent in the interest in 'national innovation systems' (see especially Lundvall, 1992). Not only was innovation placed at the heart of industrial policy, but it was recognised that the main contribution of policy would be to alter the framework conditions governing the learning capacities of individual firms as well as their mutual interactions. Embodying both a network focus and a recognition of the primacy of innovation, the 'national innovation system' concept had already significantly influenced industrial policy prior to the cluster concept. For example, as part of a national industrial policy in the UK during the early 1990s, the Technology Foresight programme adopted a more systematic approach to identifying the country's key policy priorities by supporting preferential scientific and technological development and an increase in the commercialisation of research and university interactions with the business community (Freeman, 1994). More direct links between cluster and industrial policy can be seen in the case of the Centre of Expertise programme in Finland, as discussed in the Tampere case study.

The intersections between industrial and science/technology policy implied by these developments make it difficult to discuss the latter as a separate policy area. For two decades, industrial and science research policies have been developing links with the latter, showing a decided shift away from support for 'blue-sky science' to encouraging the innovation interactions between existing research providers and business communities (Peterson and Sharp, 1998). As already noted, the focus on innovation has been a critical part of science policy, as demonstrated by the profusion and regional focus of innovation support policies over the past decade. This has been most visibly manifested in regional innovation strategies to support the emergence of economic environments more conducive to encouraging innovative enterprises (Downes *et al*, 2000). Often financed through the European Union, many of these policies have presaged cluster policy by their combination of existing policy resources within a single strategic framework in support of the local innovation system. They have been characterised by a changing mode of public sector intervention, shifting from what Nauwelærs (2001) has described as support for *physical* capital (such as equipment) and *human* capital (skills training) to *social* capital, especially the relationships between the major innovation actors in the local economy. Indeed, several policies formed the basis for later cluster policies, as has been the case in Limburg, as discussed in the chapter in this volume.

Perhaps more significantly, cluster policy has a strong foundation in recent trends in spatial development policy. Overall, it can be argued that cluster policy has been more commonly used to promote local rather than national competitive advantage as an objective of policy (Raines, 2001b). At least in Western Europe, cluster policies have typically been associated with local economic development: for example, such policies have been initiated or are under serious consideration by regional policy ministries in Finland, France, Norway and the UK. In this, cluster policy has perhaps acted as a kind of 'trojan horse', bringing the insights of other policy areas into spatial policy. However, the cluster concept has lent itself well to spatial development in large part because of recent trends in regional economic policy relating to the regional environment, the regional business community, the relationship between that community and the environment, and lastly, the delivery of policy. Each of these should be considered in turn.

First, policy interventions in support of the regional economy have adopted new ways of understanding and influencing the *regional environment*. Increasingly, policies envisage regions as "unique set(s) of relational assets" (Lagendijk, 1999b, p.111), in which policy should focus as much on the interaction between the existing assets as on the improvement of each asset in isolation. More traditional forms of intervention have typically concentrated on the attraction, development or retention of a specific asset. What is more significant now is how policy can embed those assets in the local economy and augment the number and value added of the linkages between those assets and the wider regional economic environment. This had already become evident with respect to policy approaches to attracting foreign investment, in which a new emphasis has been placed on increasing the value of foreign investment projects to the local economy by improving the links between investors and local suppliers (Brown and Raines, 2000).

Second, regional policy has developed new targets within the *regional business community*. Greater attention has been given in policy initiatives over the past decade to indigenous SME development (OECD, 2000a). The focus on SMEs and new business start-ups reflects both a recognition of the significant role of SMEs in employment creation as well as a desire to avoid regional economic dependency through support for large investment projects. It can be seen in the profusion of programmes to encourage entrepreneurship, facilitate new firm formation and assist small enterprise growth. It is also evident in the shift in FDI policy towards diffusing the benefits of large investors through supply chains often consisting of locally-based SMEs. This emphasis on SMEs has led directly to cluster policies concentrating on SME development (the 'SME networking' model of cluster policy defined by Boekholt and Thuriaux (1999)).

Third, the *relationships between businesses and their regional environment* are being considered in new ways by spatial policy (Asheim, 1999b). The sources of regional competitiveness have been increasingly cast in terms of the knowledge and innovation capacity of local enterprises. As already noted, a more sophisticated distinction has been made between *knowledge generation* – which has traditionally been supported through the RTD measures of national industrial policy – and *learning* – which entails examining the local systems supporting such learning, not just in individual businesses but in the wider economy. The policy focus on what makes enterprises more innovative has prompted questions about the external environmental conditions which support innovation. It also underlies an emerging conception of regional development as a self-regenerating set of processes that influences enterprise innovation, both individually and collectively as industries.

Lastly, it also demonstrates a growing interest in the role of strong, *regionalised policy institutions* as factors in regional economic development. In particular, it has been linked to the rise of regional development agencies in Western Europe and a shift in the institutions responsible for regional development (Morgan, 1996). Over the past few decades in Europe, there has been a clear trend towards the decentralisation of regional development policy-making. While funding has continued to be centrally provided, more scope has been given to 'bottom-up' approaches to local economic development, in large part because there is greater recognition that local institutions are often in a better position to determine local economic needs (Halkier and Danson, 1997). It is not surprising then that many local economic development agencies have been at the forefront of designing and implementing cluster policies (for example, in Scotland, as discussed in more detail later).

Such an integrated, 'bottom-up' approach to spatial development, often encapsulated by cluster policy, owes much of its origins to the role of the Structural Funds. At least in Europe, EU regional policy has been a major factor in the adoption of a more integrated, strategy-based approach towards regional development (Bachtler and Taylor, 1997). The way in which EU Structural Funds strategies combine different types of policies around a hierarchy of priorities and overall aims provided a model for the development of cluster strategies. Indeed, in the case of some regions (notably North-Rhine Westphalia in this volume), the Structural Funds programme has been a critical part of cluster policy. Moreover, in meeting EU requirements on designing and operating Structural Funds strategies, public agencies in regions have been making greater use of partnerships between different economic development agents, again, laying the groundwork for cluster policy-making.

Part 2: Practice

Chapter 4

Arve Valley

François Josserand

Introduction

Cluster policy is at an early stage in France. Until recently clusters of small and medium-sized firms were not identified as such or recognised as a relevant specific object of economic policy. However, a wide range of policy instruments have been used at different levels to target areas where small and medium-sized firms working in the same or in similar sectors are concentrated. Therefore, one could argue that significant elements of cluster policy have been pursued for some time already, particularly after the decentralisation laws of the early 1980s which created regional assemblies with significant responsibilities in economic development. From this time, awareness grew among policy-makers that large areas of French industry were being threatened by the rise of competition from emerging economies, and that preventive action had to be taken.

In the mid 1990s, there was growing interest within the economic and spatial planning unit of the central State, DATAR, in cluster policies. French policy-makers somewhat 'rediscovered' the traditional concentration of small and medium-sized firms which had long existed in French regions. It was reckoned that these areas were a relevant scale for economic policy, in large part out of a sense that France was lagging behind other European countries – particularly Italy – in local economic development.

The Arve Valley defines itself as one of the premier 'industrial districts' in France as well as the world's leading area for the metal-cutting industry. It is a good illustration of how cluster policies have been undertaken in France. First, for more than a decade, local authorities have been actively pursuing local economic policies aimed at small and medium-sized firms and which take into account the specific nature of the local economic fabric. Second, the cluster project submitted by local policy-makers in the Valley has been selected by DATAR in its pilot operation of cluster policy.

The Arve Valley is an area of about 30 kilometres in diameter between Geneva and the Mont-Blanc chain of mountains. It contains 60,000 inhabitants in 17 *communes* [towns]. The valley is well located on one of the main north-south European motorway systems, at a very short distance from Switzerland and Italy. Geneva and Annecy airports and fast-speed train (TGV) stations are close by. According to the latest national census, the four *cantons* (the administrative unit immediately above the town level) of the Valley have seen their population increase by between 7 and 14 percent from 1990 to 1999. The population of the Valley is expected to grow through to 2010.

The economic structure of the Arve Valley cluster is specialised around one sector and its related activities. Although there is a wide range of techniques in working with metal, they are all based on the same industrial basic set of production processes. As a result, firms tend to cooperate only in peripheral activities such as transport, export, training, market sharing, etc. In other words, there is no vertical integration of labour aimed at manufacturing a unique product and little joint RTD takes place. This is not the case for all the clusters in France, where firms tend to work at all stages of the value chain.

The exceptional specialisation of the economic fabric in the Arve Valley has its origins in the timepiece industry of neighbouring Switzerland. The process started in the 18th century with farmers becoming part-time craftsmen and working as sub-contractors. Such production gradually became a major industry in the 19th century with the foundation of the Royal School of Clock Making in the Valley, the industrialisation of craft techniques and the development of a cheap local source of hydro-electric energy using the Arve River. In the 20th century, increasing demand from aircraft and car manufacturers, as well as the electrical and photographical sectors, created a boom in the area. The metal cutting industry grew with these sectors.

The Arve Valley is now a major industrial area and the base for over 800 SMEs dedicated to specialist sub-contracting for the industry. The Valley has the largest concentration of screw-cutting companies in the world. Sixty-five percent of the French metal-cutting industry is concentrated in the Arve Valley with an overall turnover of 7.5bn Francs (€1.14bn).[13] Of the 17,000 staff in the screw-cutting industry in France, about 12,600 work in the Haute-Savoie *département*.[14] The main characteristic of the Valley is its fabric of family-based SMEs. Few of the 800 firms in the industry have more than 20 employees.

The context of the cluster approach

Mechanical components produced in the Arve Valley can be found in a wide range of products, from high technology innovations to everyday objects (cars, electric goods, telephones, etc). Under the impact of technological progress and high demand, companies have specialised in activities complementary to bar turning. Consequently there is a very broad spectrum of know-how in the complex assembly of metal pieces undertaken in the Valley. The main activity of over 470 companies is the mass production of a diverse range of mechanical parts. A large series of small components are made by turning, grinding and boring bars of metal. The turned parts can go through mechanical finishing operations (surfacing, rolling, roller finishing, sizing and grinding) and/or heat and surface treatment to obtain specific mechanical properties, for instance to improve their resistance to corrosion. Other firms specialise in welding, spring manufacturing boiler-making and alternative manufacturing processes such as stamping and cutting using presses or lasers from metal sheets and trips. In addition, many firms also work with plastics (which is injected, extruded or heat-shaped). Overall, specialist companies provide assembly services for mounting together mechanical, electrical and electronic devices and industrial equipment.

A wide range of policy actors play a role in the economic development of the Arve Valley metal-cutting cluster. On the one hand, their actions can be identified as cluster policy (although the term has been translated into the French *Système Productif Localisé*) in the case of the pilot cluster policy promoted by the central government agency DATAR. On the other hand, the economic measures targeted at SMEs are traditional local economic development policies promoted by local authorities at various levels in partnerships with a number of other actors such as chambers of commerce. Although these have not been seen as cluster policy as such, they are very much tailored to the specific economic fabric and needs of the Valley. In addition, for some policy-makers in the Arve Valley in particular, there is a real understanding that the Valley is one among many existing (or emerging) clusters found in France which could benefit from sharing experience and examples of good practice.

The wider national policy context is relevant here. The design and implementation of public policies in France are very much determined by the complex institutional pattern of government. For mainly historical reasons, several different levels of government have shared responsibility for economic development in the same geographical areas so their remit sometimes overlap. In consequence, there is a growing emphasis on all policy-making levels cooperating in a partnership approach. The aim has been to ensure that the tangle of administrative divisions does not prevent policy-makers from working together and targeting areas which do not necessarily fit with their own geographical remit. For instance, the 'Arve Valley' itself is not a local administrative division, but an area covered by several different layers of administration. However, since it is a relevant area for conducting economic policy, it has been chosen as the target for economic policy, or as it is officially called, a 'functional economic area' (or *bassin* in French).

With a long tradition of policy centralisation, the state has played a very important role and continues to do so, either though its central forward planning unit, DATAR, or locally via deconcentrated services, ie. the local representatives of its various departments. However, the regional level is of growing importance, mainly due an accelerated process of decentralisation initiated by laws passed in the early 1980s.

The key regional development organisation in France as a whole is the Delegation for Spatial Development and Regional Action (*Délégation à l'Aménagement du Territoire et à l'Aide*, DATAR). This agency has responsibility for local development within a wider remit and undisputed primacy in spatial planning policies. Often acting as a think-tank, its role has been to propose innovative policies and test their relevance before they can be more generally applied. Since the early 1980s, many pilot schemes have been launched in support of local economic growth and job creation. These experimental projects are often meant to be models which can then be adapted at the local level. Indeed, DATAR has built upon lessons learnt from recent projects to launch its recent pilot cluster policies. However, it only started to think actively about promoting cluster policies in the mid-1990s, leading to the launch of two calls for projects in 1998 and 1999.

At the same time, the local policy context has been equally important in determining policy directions in the Arve Valley. During the administrative decentralisation of the 1980s, when 22 regions were created in an attempt to bring together the 90 *départements* which have existed since the French Revolution, several policy areas were devolved to the regions and local economic development became part of their remit. The Arve Valley is part of the Rhône-Alpes Region, largest of all regions in France as well as the second richest (after the Ile-de-France region). However, the *départements* still play some role in local economic development. Although their exact remit is based on a legal framework, there remains considerable variation in the degree to which they are involved in local economic development.

Within the Arve Valley, local organisations and government structures have been central to the development of a cluster approach. Prominent among these is the Intermunicipal Association of the Mid-Arve Valley (*Syndicat Intercommunal de la Moyenne Vallée de l'Arve*, SIDEMVA), a single-purpose intermunicipal association" (*Syndicat intercommunal à vocation unique*)[15] bringing together 17 towns of the Arve Valley. SIDEMVA was set up in 1995 to assist businesses and co-ordinate local development action plans.

Similarly, the Employer's Association for Bar-Turners and Cylindrical Screw Cutters was created in 1897; it is one of the oldest trade associations in France. The S.N.DEC is the successor of this first organisation and pursues the same goals and tasks, namely promoting the screw-cutting industry. Significantly, the S.N.DEC is located in Cluses, in the heart of the Arve Valley, although it is a national association representing the whole French screw-cutting industry. The S.N.DEC brings together the resources, skills and experience of SMEs and provides support to its members in all aspects of their work: finance and regulation, international markets, putting clients and suppliers in touch with one another, professional training, etc. The Associations has a number of functions. First, it gathers and disseminates information for the profession, such as statistics, economic analyses, market and labour cost studies, long-term surveys, etc. Second, it is charged with raising the profile of the screw-cutting industry through circulating brochures about its techniques, products and services, taking part in national and international exhibitions and conferences, and arranging meetings between screw-cutting professionals and suppliers and clients, consular officials, representatives of technical centres, etc. Lastly, it acts as a spokesperson for the industry *vis-à-vis* the press, government authorities and legal bodies at both regional and national level.

The last key institution is the *Centre Technique de l'Industrie du Décolletage* (C.T.DEC), an industrial technical centre whose mission is to promote technical progress, improvements in productivity and the quality of products manufactured by the screw-machining industry. It is divided into six operational departments: quality assurance; metrology; materials; productivity; automation; and technical information. The centre provides technical assistance to local companies though a wide range of quality control, productivity improvement and information services. Companies regularly use the design and engineering equipment and videoconferencing facilities. The Centre handles technology transfer for firms based in the Valley and perhaps most importantly, offers vocational training to their employees: on average, more than 2,000 trainees take part in one of its 400 classes each year.

The C.T.DEC was founded in 1962 by a few employers, in response to a French law passed in 1948 encouraging employers to create 'industrial technical centres' for their sector. The law established a unique but complex funding process whereby industrial firms received the revenue of a tax on their sales. The law also ensured that the Technical Centres would respond to the demands and needs of firms in each sector. The management board include a variety of public and private partners, including representatives from firms. Although the C.T.DEC initially met with both resistance or indifference from the large majority of firms in the Valley, the Centre gradually managed to establish itself as key instrument for the industry. It is now widely used by and recognised as one of the most successful of all the 'technical centres' in France.

Cluster approach and economic policy tools at the national level

French SMEs suffer from a double handicap: they are in general smaller than their German counterparts and maintain fewer linkages between each other than their Italian neighbours (Aniello and le Galès, 2001). Therefore they tend to lack resources and are often isolated, especially subcontracting firms which face strong product pricing and quality pressures from their customers. In this context, public policies aimed at strengthening emerging or existing clusters provide an adequate solution by encouraging cooperation between firms and the sharing of resources and dedicated services.

Traditionally, public policies to support SMEs in France have been based on generic policy tools such as innovation support, training and financial aid. They have often neglected the spatial dimension: the fact that many SMEs belong to a spatial unit and have strong relationships with other local firms. They have targeted individual firms rather than the systems or networks in which they fit, although these are often the real production units. In this context, policy-makers have begun to supplement this set of policies with other tools that could support the growth and development of existing clusters. This required clusters to be recognised as a relevant focus for economic policy and specific policy tools to be tailored for different types of clusters.

DATAR has undertaken work on cluster policy since 1995. The general perception in government was that France was lagging behind Italy with respect to the latter's industrial districts. However, it was not possible to import this model directly. Policy-makers at the national level did not want their policies to be seen as 'technocratic', imposed from the top down without consultation with local actors. As a result, DATAR aimed to work at all stages with people 'in the field', determined that its work should be as inclusive as possible. The motive was to ensure that French regions would no longer be seen as a homogeneous receptacle into which regional policies could be 'poured' from the top down. Instead, national policy-makers should recognise that regions have specialised in particular economic sectors and policies should be adapted accordingly.

More importantly, DATAR saw its emerging cluster policies as part of wider action to reconstruct French territory, encouraging its segregated administrative units to join together to address economic issues at the most relevant scale, rather than independently (and occasionally in competition). Historically, French territory has been broken up and policy making has sometimes suffered from the excessive division of territory into different layers of government. Indeed, new layers were added in the process of decentralisation in the early 1980s. New regional assemblies and a great number of public agencies were created and superimposed on the previous administrative divisions. These have not faded away but have often been stoutly defended by their elected members, such as the General Council and the mayors of the French *communes*. The problem is that they did not encompass a very relevant scale for economic policy anymore, as radical changes have occurred in the French economic and demographic structure in the period since they were first set up.

DATAR regarded its emerging cluster policy as part of an overall attempt to rebuild French 'territories' and redefine the nature of the broad concept of *aménagement du territoire*. While DATAR has drawn some of its rationale from both the literature on cluster policy and the industrial districts of the 'Third' Italy, it has decided to coin its own term to refer to what is sees as the very specific nature of the networks of SMEs in France: Local Productive Systems (*Systèmes Productifs Localisés*,[16] or SPLs). The main reason for not using the term 'cluster' is that it does not explicitly include the notion of 'territory'. French SPLs have a strong historical background and a set of economic traditions which must be taken into account as they have a deep impact on the economic structure of their functional economic areas. However, the existing term 'districts' was not appropriate as French SPLs are not typically organised around villages or towns as in Italy. French SPLs precisely lack the strong linkages found between firms and other actors in Italian districts. The term SPL is meant to emphasise the need for reconstructing and building up for the first time these links among small firms and policy-makers.

DATAR decided that clusters were useful tools to understand the development of SMEs, an innovative approach to local economic and spatial planning policy and a new scale at which these policies could be implemented. The first step was to identify networks of firms in order to be better prepared to select applications and make sure the funding would go to the most relevant projects. In 1997, studies were commissioned of TECSA Consultants and the *Institut de Recherche Economique sur la Production et le Développement* at the University Pierre Mendès France in Grenoble. They showed that the SPL concept had empirical roots, provided that it referred to a wider notion than the Italian 'industrial districts' in order to take into account the specificity of French SMEs. Around 80 clusters and another 40 labour market areas with clustering features were identified and formed the basis of DATAR's work on clusters. Three categories of SPLs were identified at the national level, based on statistical data and opinions gathered from the regions: established/recognised SPLs; emerging/virtual SPLs; and non-cluster concentrations of SMEs.

In 1998, DATAR launched a call to tender for projects supporting the SPLs to encourage the creation or consolidation of SME networks at the local level and strengthen the local public bodies which participated. The objective for DATAR was not only to provide support for project managers, but undertake a census and inventory of the 'existing productive systems working with this logic on the French territory', in other words to identify clusters. This is the reason why the call to tender welcomed projects coming both from mature/existing and emerging SPLs. The underlying objective of this overview was to assess the real economic impact and potential of SPLs on the local economy, and the case for supporting them. Out of the 124 applications which were submitted to the *préfectures* (the bodies representing the central State, both in the *départements* and in the regions), 60 were selected by an *ad hoc* interministerial committee.

Open tendering was preferred to other methods to select projects. In the experience of policy-makers at DATAR, it was the only procedure that really put actors into motion and created competition between territories/regions, as opposed to pilot operations directed from the top down. The latter were too often tacked onto local economic structures which were not prepared to receive them, merely acting as an economic salve that did not change behaviour in depth. This illustrated the fact that DATAR has tried to avoid a mere technocratic approach and involved local decision-makers on the ground as much as possible.

The main types of projects to support SPLs were the following:

- *economic and spatial analysis*: identification of the main growth/development areas in cluster areas; search for new markets; detection of potential partnerships;
- *resources sharing*: joint purchase and use of machinery, laboratories and production units; bulk buying of raw materials, machinery and services; sharing of skills, know-how and human resources between firms;
- *marketing*: creation of common commercial structures (or sharing of marketing staff); creation of common brands; export drives; creation of websites to provide a common 'shop window' for the cluster; participation in commercial exhibition and conferences;
- *training*: identification of common skill shortages and needs for personnel; creation of training centres or enhancement of existing facilities; information campaigns for young people to increase their awareness of the jobs available in the clusters; and
- *innovation*: common measures in research and development and technology transfer; linkages with existing public and semi-public research and development institutions; systematic link-up with public institutional partners such as ANVAR (the national innovation agency), DRIRE (*Direction Régionale de l'Industrie, de la Recherche et de l'Environnement*, the deconcentrated representative of the Departments of Industry, the Environment and Research), DRRTs (*Délégations régionales à la recherche et à la technologie*, the administrative bodies in charge of the decentralised actions of the State in research, technology and innovation as well as scientific and technology education), CRITTs (*Centres Régionaux d'Innovation et de Transfert de Technologie*, technology and research centres with the same remit but at the regional level); and promotion of economic commercial and technological intelligence.

The project selected by DATAR for the Arve Valley was submitted by SIDEMVA in 1998. It was one of 60 successful projects out of 124 put forward by various local policy-makers. The project, entitled *Development and Prospects for the Industrial District of the Arve Valley*, mainly provided support for the 'enterprise clubs' created by the OSST in 1997 in telecommunication wiring, medical equipment and international commercial intelligence. The project lasted one year and it was managed by the SIDEMVA. The 800 firms and 12,000 jobs of the metal-cutting industry in the Valley were officially targeted. All the cluster's local partners were involved in the project, i.e. the S.N.DEC, the C.T.DEC, the OSST and the Chamber of Commerce for the Haute-Savoie *département*.

One can see that this pilot project supported by DATAR was mainly exploratory, given the limited duration and funding made available. One of the main underlying objectives was to raise awareness among local policy-makers and contribute to building a sense of community in the Valley while making more tangible at the local level the concept of SPL coined by DATAR to describe the specific nature of clusters in France.

This is the reason why many local actors claim that they did not wait for DATAR before coming together to work out a common strategy for the Valley. The metal-cutting trade has been organised for decades in its employers' association which again is based locally. Metal-cutters are themselves very jealous of their know-how and competitive edge and proud of the common resources some of them have managed to set up with great efforts, such as the C.T.DEC. Paradoxically, it took more than a decade for this centre to be accepted by local entrepreneurs after it was established in the 1960s. Therefore local actors can sometimes feel puzzled by what they see as an essentially bureaucratic superimposition of a the new label of 'SPL' on the work which they have been conducting for years. Besides, a few leading personalities within public actors such as Jean-Claude Léger, the mayor of Cluses, who understood early on the case for an active cluster policy in the Valley and campaigned locally for this objective. Therefore local actors generally welcomed the work done by DATAR but continue to feel slightly remote. In addition, local actors can disagree with the focus of DATAR on both existing and emerging clusters. They reckon the efforts should be focused on real growth areas but which still need public support to maintain their competitive edge, as is the case for the Arve Valley, rather than on the declining traditional activities which are also supported by SPL actions.

Policy at the regional level

The pilot operation launched by DATAR came on top of regional and local initiatives. Networks of SMEs had often already been identified locally by policy-makers in different sub-national tiers of government. Regional economic frameworks have also provided localised support for cluster development. As a result, the SPLs now supported by DATAR have been targeted by the regions as part of their economic development policies, as well as by other local authorities and public bodies such as the *départements* and their economic development agencies and local councils, particularly through intermunicipal associations (*syndicat intercommunal*). Although not specifically termed 'cluster policy', the approach contains many similar elements. In the case of the Arve Valley, the most relevant policy instrument is the local 'contract' (*contrats de bassin* and *contrat global*).

This scheme is effectively a written agreement signed for a period of five years by the regional authority and other policy and economic players, among which is the *Conseil Général* (i.e. the local authority at the *département* level) and local authorities coming together within an intermunicipal association. The aim is to build a real development strategy for the medium to long term and ensure that it is endorsed by a wide range of key actors, superseding traditional local administrative borders and promoting cooperation. Local contracts provide funding for measures aimed at improving the infrastructure for local economic development, but do not target firms as such. The main themes are those of traditional regional policy, mainly training, innovation, international market development and business incubation. This instrument dates back to the early 1990s but was redesigned in the mid-1990s in the Rhône-Alpes Region in order to adopt a less sector specific and more strategic approach. The Region was to rationalise the various tools of economic development it had on offer for local authorities. The new 'global contracts' (*contrat global*) are meant to consider economic areas as a whole by supporting a wide range of projects from public and private partners within a pre-defined geographical areas – the main selection criteria being their potential impact and their coherence with the overall strategy. The Region funds up to 30 percent of the overall sum of a global contract, though the exact proportion varies depending on projects and resources locally available.

The local contract covering the Arve Valley was signed following the economic crisis of 1992-93, which significantly affected the Valley. Industry suffered considerably with many firms closing down. Local councillors decided to seize the opportunity provided by the local contract scheme proposed by the Rhône-Alpes Region. The mayor of Cluses – the main town in the Valley and the birthplace of the sector – played a key role in bringing local towns together to sign a local contract for the Arve Valley in 1995. The scheme was co-funded by the Rhône-Alpes Region, the *département* of Haute-Savoie and the towns of the Valley brought together within SIDEMVA. Seventeen million francs (€2.6 million) were invested in five areas: technological innovation; economic intelligence; training; branding and marketing; and strategic planning. The underlying objective was to ensure that local firms would have a strong sense of ownership of the programme and the projects supported. Table 4.1 illustrates the different key components of the contract as it related to cluster development.

Table 4.1: **Components of the local economic contract in the Arve Valley**

Themes	Measures	Leading agency	Source of funds
Technology	• Skills centre in mounting-assembling and in the design of industrial products • "Just-in-time" production service for firms • Videoconferencing with 24-hour access	*C.T.DEC* *(Centre Technique de l'Industrie du Décolletage)*	Rhône-Alpes Region (c30 %)
Economic Intelligence	• Creation of the Strategic Intelligence Observatory for the subcontracting industry (OSST). Services include: targeted news service; newsletter; thematic club meetings	*Association Arve Stratégie* (employers' associations): S.N.DEC and independent employers) and help from the C.T.DEC and the Chambers of commerce	Département of Haute-Savoie (c30 %)
Training	• Training provided for low skilled workers • System of reference describing all the skills needed in the metal-cutting industry	*Association pour la Valorisation des connaissances* (Association for the Improvement of Skills)	SIDEMVA (c30 %)
Public Relations Marketing	• Creation and promotion of brand (logo, etc.) • Directory of subcontracting firms • News bulletin • Brochure • Attendance at exhibitions	*SIDEMVA* (intermunicipal association)	
Strategic Planning	• Creation of the "French Club of Industrial Districts" • Preparation of the Global Development Contract	*SIDEMVA* (intermunicipal association)	Various partners: State; Chambers of Commerce; C.T.DEC; S.N.DEC; independent employers (c10 %)

The *technological innovation* part of the contract included three main projects: creating 'skills centres' in metal mounting and assembling techniques and in industrial design to encourage the diversification of techniques and skills in the industry; encouraging the use of consultancy services to help for firms introduce new methods in management and production quality; and providing self-service, round-the-clock access to videoconference facilities.

The *economic intelligence* aspect was entrusted to the newly-created 'Arve Stratégie' association, bringing together the two main unions of employers as well as independent employers. Its responsibility was to create a 'Strategic Intelligence Observatory for the Subcontracting Industry' (*Observatoire Stratégique de la Sous-Traitance*, OSST), a small organisation providing technological and market intelligence for local firms".

Training was also a key aspect of the local contract. This theme is particularly relevant in the industry as firms face great difficulties to recruit workers with the appropriate specialised skills. The objective was to train employees with low skills and to define a benchmark identifying the exact sets of skills needed in the metal-cutting industry.

As part of its *public relations and marketing* remit, SIDEMVA was given the task of creating a brand name and logo for the Arve Valley – renamed 'Technic Valley' – in order to provide a common identity which could easily be adopted by local firms. A complete directory of subcontracting firms was established and has been regularly updated. Last, brochures, newsletters and bulletins were published and widely circulated.

SIDEMVA is also responsible for *strategic planning* within the local contract. Concretely, this mainly included the creation of networks of existing clusters in France to exchange best practice. This 'French Club of Industrial Districts' was officially launched in July 1998 as a non-profit association.

The creation of the OSST as part of the local contract is particularly interesting in terms of policy to encourage firms to cluster. It is very difficult for SMEs to take a broader view of developments in markets and technology, given their lack of resources in terms of time, expertise and funds. Policy-makers identified more than a decade ago the need to provide firms with strategic intelligence. An organisation was needed to help local firms anticipate rapid changes in the industry and maintain their competitive edge.

The OSST was created to monitor the business environment in the metal-cutting industry. Its purpose was to scrutinise rapidly-changing market trends and technological developments and circulates its conclusions to subcontracting firms in the Arve Valley. The objective has been to help SMEs maintain their competitive edge from a technological, commercial and economic point of view. This small organisation is available for any firm working as a subcontractor in the metal-cutting industry, and in particular for those located within one of the 17 communes of SIDEMVA. Another underlying aim has been to encourage greater partnership between suppliers and customers working in the same sector but using different techniques, particularly as far the management of human resources and use of information technologies are concerned.

The OSST publishes thematic newsletters reflecting economic trends in the industry. A targeted news service has also been set up to distribute news on crucial commercial and technological changes. Last, regular conferences are organised for local managers, focusing on more in-depth issues affecting firms in the industry. Alongside, the 'Enterprise clubs' the OSST has set up, these are meant to provide a platform for key players to discuss common issues.

Conclusions: a mature Local Productive System, not quite a cluster yet

The Arve Valley fits well with the description of cluster and the 'diamond' model of Michael Porter. Its strength lies in its accumulated technical know-how which has reinforced its competitiveness at the world level. However, the 'cluster' is complicated by its anchorage to a very specific territory, a complex set of historical, economic, political and even anthropological factors which operate in the Arve Valley. These factors have been real strengths for the Valley but at the same time they can represent future weaknesses and must be addressed by policy-makers to ensure the success of their policies.

This is where the term of SPL coined by DATAR is particularly relevant. Of all the projects supported by DATAR as part of its pilot operations, the Arve Valley is indeed the largest economic area targeted in terms of firms and employees. It is seen as a typical example of mature SPL, as opposed to other emerging SPLs targeted by DATAR. Yet, the Valley cannot be considered as a proper industrial district, since there is very little room for the kind of cooperation and networking seen in Italy, collaboration between firms which essentially compete with each other. Indeed, many policy-makers have noted that firms would rather lose a market than re-subcontract part of it to their competitors. This is only partly explained by the local culture in the valleys of the département of Haute-Savoie, where people have traditionally been regarded as particularly individualistic. This is due to historical reasons associated with farming conditions in the Alps as the Arve Valley has traditional family-based firms which compete with each other to win market share. While it has been an asset as firms have worked to renew constantly their skills and techniques, the mindset is gradually becoming more and more counterproductive as the economic context is changing.

In this context, it is easy to understand why the most crucial issue for the success of policies is how to get firms themselves involved. Since there is initially no real demand for public policies, firms have had to be convinced that the instruments offered are useful to them. Nevertheless, firms have started to recognise that they form a community. They have been sharing common resources such as the technical centre for some time, and new ones have recently been introduced such as the Strategic Intelligence Observatory. In addition, a new generation of entrepreneurs is gradually taking over in the Valley. The new managers are often more educated than the previous generation and often have international experience. They have a clearer understanding of the challenges ahead and do not share their predecessors' hesitations in working together. Still, most entrepreneurs do not appear prepared to be involved in projects in which they do not see any short-term benefit, such as the technical help they obtain from the C.T.DEC. Although many have taken part in the activities organised by the new Strategic Intelligence Observatory, progress has been slow and notable among those entrepreneurs who are already the most proactive and work in leading sectors (i.e. not those who would benefit most from using this tool). The same assessment can be made of the public relations campaign: while many firms now display the 'Technic Vallée' on their brochures, many are still reluctant to be associated with any sort of common identity, as they cannot see the immediate benefits for them.

In this context, the DATAR pilot project has been, to some extent, a re-branding of existing policies and tools for economic development. The technical centre for the metal-cutting industries dates back to the 1960s and the chambers of commerce have been working on marketing for more than a decade. Economic strategies have been designed and implemented at the local level by all the actors in collaboration throughout the 1990s, although they have never been called cluster or SPL policies as such. Hence, many local actors – for whom SPL policy has been presented from the top down – do not really see what is new and different about the policy. For them, DATAR seems to have suddenly 'discovered' clusters. It remains to be seen how the pilot policies will be pursued and taken over by local actors, notably as part of the Global Contract for the Valley.

The long tradition of very specialised work in one industrial sector has resulted in a concentration of unique skills. At the same time, the Valley is still largely dependant on this industrial sector, which makes it more vulnerable to economic threats. Some efforts have been made by policy-makers to enrich the economic fabric of the Valley but these are still in their infancy. A limited number of firms have tried to diversify their range of skills and widen their range of products. The more widespread response for entrepreneurs has been to become more specialised in specific types of skills and products, in order to maintain their position on the markets. This individualist strategy has worked up to a point but it presents many dangers for the future as emerging countries gradually acquire the skills available in the Valley and become able to offer products of comparable quality at a lower cost. Additional skills and industrial processes such as surface and heat treatments, mounting and assembling as well as plastic moulding are particularly crucial in preserving the Valley's competitiveness.

Ownership transition is also a crucial factor for the future of the metal-cutting industry. The problem of how ownership of these firms is passed to a new generation of entrepreneurs will have a great impact on the industry itself. Increasingly, entrepreneurs are deciding to leave their firms and not finding qualified managers to take over. The traditional pattern of family-based firms longer exists as few are taking over their parents' business, as has happened in the past. For small firms, the material and the techniques used are usually ageing and located in facilities which are no longer inadequate (the workshops are traditionally attached to house). As mergers and buyouts increase, the future of these small firms is uncertain. For larger firms (with 100 staff or more), the main issue of concern is the arrival of new managers who regard them primarily as a good investment opportunity. Decision-making for these firms is often no longer located in the Valley, creating longer-term problems for their sustainable development.

Last, one of the main threats for the Arve Valley is the scarce availability of a sufficiently numerous workforce. The French metal-cutting industry suffers from a poor image among the young when the latter decide on what kind of education, general or technical, they will follow at school. Far too few students are being recruited by the technical schools and trained to be metal cutters, creating tensions in the labour market.

Notes

[13] All figures are provided by the Bank of France, unless otherwise stated.

[14] Source: National screw-cutting association *(Syndicat National du Décolletage)*.

[15] An institutional framework created to encourage neighbouring town councils to work together to deliver common services to their constituents, mainly utilities such as waste collection, water provision, but also to manage specific projects which are part of regional economic policies such as the *contrat de bassin* described hereafter.

[16] Later renamed *"Systèmes Productifs Locaux"*.

Chapter 5

Limburg

Mary Louise Rooney

Introduction

Dutch industrial policy has supported cluster development for the past decade or so. As with many countries supporting cluster development, is based strongly on the cluster model put forward by Porter (1990a), which views supporting as a method of non-interventionist assistance for business development and innovation. At the same time, the Province of Limburg has also pursued a cluster development approach as part of an innovation policy framework, the Regional Technology Plan (RTP). Although not directly linked with national industrial policy support for clusters, various influences have been taken on board in the development of the RTP.

Clusters in the Limburg context are part of a five-step process to encourage companies to become more innovative. The underlying philosophy is that for companies, notably small suppliers, to survive in the increasingly competitive global market, they have to be able to offer a unique and competitive product or combination of skills. The local economy in Limburg, with its strong industrial base, contains many small companies which supply component parts to the region's large equipment manufacturers, creating a regional dependency on these large firms, not only in terms of the number they employ in the area, but also the number of small local firms. However, the development of unique products and the acquisition of new skills is something which many firms, in particular SMEs, find difficult to achieve alone. Clusters are seen as one regional solution to encouraging innovation in local firms, enabling them to remain competitive whilst at the same time, providing them with the scope to increase their customer base. Specialist knowledge is seen as the way forward for these firms, who will have difficulty competing on price alone in the global marketplace. The Province of Limburg demonstrates clustering on a very small scale, adopting some of the basic theories about clusters to their own requirements.

Context of the cluster approach

The Province of Limburg, with a population of around 1.1 million, is one the most densely populated of the twelve Dutch provinces (Province of Limburg, 2000a). Bordering both Belgium and Germany it has an optimal geographic location for export activity. Mining activity dominated the economy in the early to mid half of the 20th century, however, as with many traditional mining areas in Europe, severe job losses were experienced in this sector between the mid 1960s and mid 1970s. National, provincial and European programmes have assisted the region to overcome some of the economic problems which arose from the job losses within the mining industry, including removing much of the disused infrastructure. The region is traditionally one of the most industrialised areas in the Netherlands and regardless of the economic changes it has had to undergo, Limburg has managed to remain a very industrialised region, at a time when industry is generally in decline both nationally and throughout the European Union. Consequently, although industrial employment decreasing nationally during the mid 1990s, it *increased* in Limburg.

Another feature of the Limburg economy is the dominance of large firms in which most of its industrial jobs are based. During the early to mid 1990s, 40 percent of employment was in companies with 500 or more employees, compared to 29 percent nationally. The large company base has a strong industrial orientation with six of the ten largest Limburg companies being manufacturing concerns (Province of Limburg, 1996b). However, during the early part of the 1990s, there was a general trend of employment losses in large companies and gains in SMEs. This was attributed to a number of reorganisations taking place in many larger firms, often with that some standard activities were contracted out to external organisations, particularly regionally-based SMEs. The contracting out resulted in an overall shift in employment from large firms to local supply-based SMEs.

Overall, the most important economic activities relate to knowledge-intensive industrial activity, the main actors dominating this field including Océ (electronic industry specialising in photocopy equipment), Nedcar (transport), DSM (chemistry) and Philips (electronics). Logistics also play a strong role in the regional economic activities, particularly around the southern city of Venlo (CEC, 2001).

At the same time, there was also a notable increase in inter-firm networking activity with a distinct supply and purchasing element. Given that the large industrial entities and their smaller regionally-based suppliers are strong elements of the local economy, there has been local government support in this process, one of the most important elements of the cluster approach in this region. The provinces current economic success lies with the industrial sector and steps are now being taken to ensure that employment within this sector remains strong. The aim of the Province is to focus on knowledge intensification within the industrial sector through various types of support, one of which involves a cluster approach.

Origins of the cluster approach

The cluster approach in Limburg is a combination of European, national and Province policy directions combining industrial and innovation (and to a certain extent, regional) policies. Cluster support takes the form of assistance for industrial innovation clusters which emerged as a Province priority under the European RTP (Regional Technology Plan) pilot programme. Although this was clearly a Province innovation policy exercise, Dutch innovation and industrial policy have strongly supported the development of clusters as far back as the early 1990s, and have also become part of the policy approach at the policy-making level of the Provinces. While national involvement was not evident in the formation of the cluster element of the RTP, the philosophy of the Dutch and Limburg approaches both emphasise innovation as an important source of competitiveness and the basis for the formation of clusters. For this reason, a brief overview of the national cluster approach is given before the distinctive Limburg approach is examined.

The national approach

The Netherlands is famed for its strong advocacy of cluster approaches within national policy, particularly in industrial and innovation policy areas. The main driver for supporting cluster development is the improvement of private sector competitiveness with resulting sustainable growth and employment effects. The synergy created by a cluster approach is viewed as necessary for companies to keep pace with the acceleration of technological development as well as a method of increasing specialisation within industry (Ministry of Economic Affairs, 1997).

Cluster policy became part of Dutch national policy following the publication of Porter's *The Competitive Advantage of Nations* (Wever and Stam, 1998). A study was published in 1990 which applied Porter's model to the Dutch economy, providing an insight into the strengths of existing clusters which had taken place without direct policy intervention (Roelandt *et al,* 1999). This initial study led to more in-depth analyses of various sectors over a number of years.

The Dutch government views future growth as being dependant on the ability of companies to respond to changes in the conditions of international competitors, with the key to national competitiveness being described as the ability to turn knowledge application into new marketable products. What is needed for this to happen is innovation, so the government is aiming to create an economic environment which fosters innovation. Although the link between innovation and cluster formation was made early on in the Dutch government's support for clusters, an OECD report reiterated this link by concluding that companies rarely innovate alone and this, mixed with the requirement to innovate in order to remain competitive, has led to a trend towards networking and cluster development (OECD, 1999). With the increasing emphasis put on innovation and technology developments for the future economic success of the Netherlands, support for clusters is one of the ways this is seen as feasible. A government policy agenda produced in 1999, outlined five basic principles summarising Dutch industrial policy (Ministry of Economic Affairs, 1999):

- it is facilitative;
- it contains no blueprints or interventionist sectoral structure policy;
- it is predominantly general;
- it is designed to promote competition, eliminate shortcomings and (inter)national distortions of competition and to realise external effects of knowledge and technology; and
- it contains dynamic, flexible policies with regular testing of the effects.

The application of knowledge and technology is being seen as an increasingly important contributor towards economic growth. Through its present industrial policy, the Dutch government is seeking a way for both to be exploited as much as possible, but rather than using an interventionist approach, it aims to achieve this by creating conditions conducive to successful enterprise and industrial innovation. Addressing the current problems facing the economy, a policy agenda has been created which addresses seven areas, one of which is 'strengthening innovative cluster policy' by (Ministry of Economic Affairs, 1999):

- closer attention to SMEs;
- coordination with (regional) initiatives;
- intensified strategic information supply; and
- innovative procurement policy.

As a result, there are numerous clusters operating nationally in the Netherlands within various sectors including construction, the chemical and paper manufacturing industries and health (Van den Hove, 1998).

The Limburg approach

Support for cluster development at Dutch national level is part of industrial policy, but it has also been pursued within the Province of Limburg as an element of innovation policy. During the mid 1990s, Limburg was one of four regions selected to create a Regional Technology Plan (RTP) as part of an EU pilot project. The goal in Limburg was to develop a structure to maximise coordination between technology development and regional potential, encompassing all innovation support measures available in the region, including those within the regional Objective 2 strategy and operated by the Province.

The RTP covered the period 1996-99 but the Province has continued to have an innovation strategy under a new programme called RIS+ (Regional Innovation Strategy), which retains the RTP philosophy. The reason why cluster formation is part of the RTP within Limburg requires a detailed explanation as it is also linked to the reason why Limburg pursued the creation of a RTP in the first place.

Cluster development within the RTP

Cluster development cannot be examined independently from the RTP because the formation of clusters in Limburg is within the framework of the RTP matrix. In order to understand the strategic and policy thinking related to clusters, it is first necessary to understand the aims and structure of the RTP. The three most prominent actors in the creation, management and implementation of the RTP (with particular emphasis on the cluster element of the plan) are: (i) the Province of Limburg and two of the main innovation policy implementation organisations; (ii) Syntens (the regional branch of a national economic development agency); and (iii) LIOF (Limburg Institute for Development and Financing).

In 1993, when Syntens had started receiving national funding to form regional clusters, Limburg was selected as one of four pilot regions, together with Lorraine (France), Wales (UK) and Halle-Leipzig-Dessau (Germany), to create a regional strategy combining regional economic and technology policy. The aim within Limburg was not the creation of a new technology policy, but rather to achieve coordination between existing resources available in the region for technology and innovation development. The Limburg RTP was created in a cooperative process involving representatives of the Province, intermediary organisations and local companies, the Provincial authorities maintaining the overall coordinating role. The first RTP pilot projects were launched in 1995 after two years of creating the RTP and work schedule. In 1996, the final RTP was completed and its implementation began.

The main aim of the original RTP was to "reinforce the level of knowledge within industrial companies in Limburg, especially SMEs, and improve their access to the knowledge and educational infrastructure and the extent to which this infrastructure meets their needs" (Province of Limburg, 1996a). Prior to its official launch, five projects were selected to pilot the RTP with the aim of testing the feasibility and practical application of various measures. The RTP which emerged from this comprised three aims and ten priorities, one of which fell under the heading of 'cooperation': this was later to develop into the cluster element of the refined RTP.

One of the aims of the RTP was to adapt to the needs of the economy and have the flexibility to make related amendments to its strategy as required. As a result, monitoring of the 1996-97 phase of implementation led to changes in the structure of the implementation framework. The result was a regrouping of the ten priorities into four activity groupings and the breaking down of the business innovation process into five components. The reason for dividing the process of innovation into its component parts was because many of the companies being assisted were already open to innovation. It became obvious to the RTP development team that another group of firms needed to be targeted, namely those not yet open to innovation. Consequently, one of the identified stages of the process was the sensitisation of companies which had no real philosophy of innovation to make them aware of the possibilities and potential benefits.

An RTP matrix was created which defined the RTP approach, combining the four newly-defined activity groupings and the five business innovation process components (Table 5.1). This was designed both to create appropriate measures in the RTP and to 'place' existing projects and measures in a wider understanding of the process of innovation.

Figure 5.1: RTP matrix in Limburg

Phases in innovation plan for companies

RTP Activity Groupings	Sensiti-sation	Access to knowledge	Improve-ment	Inno-vation	Coope-ration
1. Knowledge in companies					
2. Knowledge transfer					
3. New business activity					
4. Flanking activities and internationali-sation					

Source: Province of Limburg (1998) *Regional Technology Plan for Limburg, RTP Report 1996-1997.*

The five stages of innovation (horizontal in the matrix) are described as:

- *sensitisation* – reaching companies which are resistant to innovation projects through promotion and awareness raising campaigns;
- *access to knowledge* – expanding the level of existing and new knowledge to make it accessible to companies;
- *improvement* – introducing forms of business management know-how which are new to the company;
- *innovation* – assisting firms to start up the process of technological innovation either using existing knowledge or through the acquisition of new knowledge; and
- *cooperation* – encouraging companies which have the technical ability to be involved in innovation clusters where, through their combined knowledge, they can undertake joint innovation projects.

Innovation clusters (described above under the heading of cooperation) have been identified as the final stage of the innovation process. Before this stage can take place, companies should already be 'innovating' through participating in measures which address the different stages of innovation. This is a genuine attempt to achieve maximum synergy through combining the work of the Province's most innovative or innovation-responsive firms. That is not to say that all of the firms involved in clusters are cutting-edge innovators, but they are willing both to cooperate with other regional firms in innovative projects and provide an important contribution towards an innovation cluster project. The formation of innovation clusters takes firms which have reached the stage of being innovators to become part of a cluster where different sources and kinds of know-how are combined to create a product or process which the involved companies could not have achieved by themselves. However, the RTP matrix had been created with the realistic expectation that not every company will have the capability of becoming part of an innovation cluster. With this in mind, assistance is available to companies at every stage of the innovation process as well as those which are able to become part of an innovation cluster.

The establishment of the RTP had provided a framework in which the various types of available support for innovation and technology measures operating within the region could be placed. In fact, no innovation and technology measures were implemented in the region outside of the RTP framework, enabling the strategic coherence of measures to be maximised. For this to function, cooperation and communication between the various programme management teams frequently took place with the purpose of creating an Innovation Project Team which could take the main role in development projects within the RTP.

At the time of the RTP creation, the Limburg economy already had a tradition of networking, although this was more of a subcontracting nature. What this structure lacked was engineering activities being part of the subcontracting arrangements, whereby specialist knowledge is held by the subcontractor SMEs rather than the large equipment manufacturers. Increasing the level of knowledge and technical ability within regional firms is seen as one of the keys to maintaining a competitive advantage over some of the lower labour cost countries. Increasing the technical ability of SMEs would contribute towards creating an interdependability between both large firms and SME suppliers which is the ultimate aim of the cooperation and cluster building element of the RTP, thereby enabling the trend towards outsourcing to be exploited.

The RTP has allowed strategic coordination of all the available measures in the region to improve the level of technology and technical ability, including European, national and Province support. While there may be coherence between cluster formation as part of Limburg innovation policy and its role within national industrial policy, these are not explicitly linked – although they do show a common rationale for cluster development, i.e. support for innovation clusters.

The Province approach adopted within the RTP was developed exclusively with regional requirements in mind by Syntens, one of the main regional actors in this approach (although part of a wider national network). One of the areas of economic development pursued by Syntens is cluster development. The cluster element of the RTP appears to have been influenced by the expertise which Syntens already had in this field, although the influence appears to be indirect. Certainly, many of the national government rationales for cluster building were used within the RTP (showing a national/regional link at the conceptual level). The type of clusters supported are specifically 'innovation clusters': based primarily on industrial innovation, there is scope for companies involved in any sector to become involved in cluster-type relationships within the RTP so long as innovation is part of the developed process.

The aim of the cluster element of the RTP was twofold: first, to improve the interdependence of OEMs (Original Equipment Manufacturers) with their component suppliers located within the Province by improving their skills and technology base, making them more competitive within a larger market; and second, to encourage clusters of businesses to work together to achieve common goals which they would not have had the expertise or resources to do themselves.

In comparison with other forms of cluster support, cluster development within the Limburg RTP is on a comparatively small scale, with 'clusters' involving as few as three firms. It is perhaps an unusual cluster approach in comparison to many of the large clusters examined elsewhere within this book; however, the creation of micro-clusters is seen as an important requirement for regional economic success. In one RTP report, clusters were defined as 'partnerships of companies focused on a product or production process (whose) purpose is to create market opportunities by improving and/or developing products' (Province of Limburg, 1998).

The cluster element of the RTP was part of a cluster development strategy which slightly pre-dated the formation of the RTP itself. As already mentioned, cluster formation was part of national policy at roughly the same time that the Province of Limburg applied for participation within the RTP pilot project. Syntens was one of the intermediaries responsible for the implementation of national policy measures, and in the early 1990s, the Venlo branch of Syntens situated in Limburg began to explore the possibility of cluster development. Although no doubt aware of the simultaneous national interest in cluster development, the reason for this exploratory work within Limburg by Syntens was driven by local considerations. The economy was in the midst of a recession in the early 1990s, and Syntens sought a new business strategy which could be used to overcome the effects of the recession at regional level. The aim was the creation of new business ideas to stimulate the economy and increase demand. The managing directors of prominent locally-based companies were invited to meet for an informal brainstorming session to generate ideas for possible solutions to overcome the effects of the recession. After a number of meetings, Syntens compiled a vision of a regional strategy to create new business demand in the region around the concept of cluster development. As the idea of clustering (or cooperation) was developed, several large firms expressed their willingness to take part in projects based on the strategy and Syntens took on the task of finding other smaller companies willing to participate. In 1993, Syntens received national funding to pursue cluster building and in the following year, became one of the partners involved in the creation of the RTP. The idea of cluster formation became one of the ten priority areas within the RTP.

Plans to expand innovation policy beyond the current scope have been put forward, to include, for example, the agro-industry, the care-sector and tourism and recreation (Province of Limburg, 2000). The Province has identified two main sources of knowledge and new expertise within the region: (i) other companies; and (ii) the education/research sector. So far, the RTP has addressed the area of knowledge transfer between companies through the development of innovation clusters with the focus on, for example, OEMs and supplier companies and the strengthening of the technical capacity for SMEs to be able to undertake research functions for OEMs as well as production activities. However, the RTP itself also addresses the importance of using local knowledge available in the education institutions as a source of technical know-how and possible expertise. The knowledge institutions in the region have been involved in the consultation process during the development of the RTP and currently have three members on the RTP pool of expertise which provides an external assessment of projects. However, their involvement as project participants has so far been very limited although the Province recognises the potential for clusters involving the education sector. This is something which will be addressed in the future. So far, from the RTP matrix, the 'knowledge in companies' and 'new business activity' strands have been the focus of implementation. 'Knowledge transfer' has been addressed so far in the form of pilot projects involving universities, higher vocational education institutions, intermediary organisations, the Chamber of Commerce and some of the large employers in the region. It is an area to be pursued further under RIS+.

The cluster approach in practice

The formation of innovation clusters within the RTP is a complicated process. Even where a feasible idea exists, company cooperation in the area of product and process design rarely occurs through the initiative of companies alone. Given that this is seen by the regional economic development actors in the region as an essential component of future economic success, this is something they are actively supporting. There are many reasons for companies not voluntarily operating together, including distrust, unwillingness to take financial risks, the prospect of negotiations concerning the concrete structure of cooperation and legal aspects concerning the distribution of eventual profits. To overcome these barriers, an intermediary facilitating the process may be necessary – to push the idea, and make companies realise the potential benefits to those involved. Strategy implementation of the Limburg RTP takes place through a variety of intermediaries, the main ones being Syntens and LIOF, who both promote the cluster measure actively and who can offer support and advice for interested companies.

Syntens and LIOF are two of the regional development actors which are involved in implementing the RTP, including the cluster formation element. Syntens plays a lead role in identifying possible clustering opportunities within the region, either through facilitating applicant firms actively searching for partners or through the identification of possible activities which they view as having clustering potential. Both approaches require good knowledge of the regional firms, individuals and funding structures. After the identification of potential partners, Syntens adopts a facilitative role, acting almost as a catalyst within the cooperation process which includes the creation of a project plan. LIOF has less of a dynamic role, but has played a strong role in the creation and mentoring of one of the region's most successful clustering ventures, namely the KIC project (discussed below).

Within the Limburg RTP, clusters of varying natures can be supported including cooperation between companies, supplier-purchaser relationships and links between companies and knowledge institutions. At the moment, the measures which are actively supported focus either on cooperation between companies to produce knowledge synergy, or supplier-purchaser relationships to improve the skills of the supplier base and promote interdependability (outsourcing).

In terms of businesses working together to encourage knowledge synergy, companies with different specialisations can work together to produce new, complex ideas. New product development and engineering solutions are becoming increasingly complex requiring a range of expertise inputs. Companies working together can produce results which would not have been possible alone.

The supplier-purchaser clustering approach is one which has seen some success in Limburg. Increasingly, OEMs no longer undertake all aspects of their business in-house, as it can be cheaper to outsource particular functions. Moreover, in an increasingly complex innovation process, some companies no longer have the resources to develop new products and processes in-house, relying instead on suppliers with the expertise to design and construct components. For example, in the car industry, component suppliers can include manufacturers of small standard components as well as manufacturers of components specific to the end product but which have been designed by the car manufacturers supplying complete sub-systems whose RTD has taken place either entirely within the supplier or jointly between the supplier and the manufacturer. This example demonstrates the level of expertise the suppliers in Limburg should be aiming to achieve.

One of the aims of the cluster strategy within the RTP is to promote interdependency between large regional manufacturers and their local suppliers in order to encourage both types of firms to stay within the region. One of the first cluster projects to be supported with this aim in mind was the KIC project (Knowledge-Intensive Industry) which ran from 1994 to 1998 (Wintjes and Cobbenhagen, 2000). Although this was a vertical collaboration it did not follow the pattern of a typical supply chain cluster, as the supplying firm was brought into the product development process. The focus of the KIC project was on a single large OEM (which produced office machinery) and its suppliers, supporting the suppliers in undertaking engineering solutions for the OEM. Syntens was involved in bringing the project partners together and securing the project funding, whilst LIOF was part of the steering group. The overall aim was to develop jointly a new photocopier, with the supplier SMEs involved in the innovation process of developing the machine components and benefiting from mentoring from the OEM and cooperation in the development of components. The KIC project involved around 40 firms, each participating in one or two of 20 micro-clusters. The firms involved were formerly 'jobbers' which – over the course of the project – became main suppliers. With the increasing levels of expertise they gained throughout the process, most have increased employment levels as a result.

Table 5.1: Selected clusters supported under the RTP in Limburg

Project Name	Basis of Support	Aim	Duration
FMIS Geleenda clustering project	RTP, ERDF, Objective 2	To develop in partnership a General and Technical Services Information System.	1999-01
Clustering project: equipment for food preparation	RTP, ERDF, Objective 2	To devise a procedure for making food preparation items and to develop equipment that will enable mass production.	1999-01
Industrial automation for ready-to-harvest mushrooms	RTP, ERDF, Objective 5b	To develop an advanced automated processing line for mushrooms preparation and packaging.	1999-01
Guidance for Objective 2 clustering projects	Provincial and ERDF	To encourage clustering and cooperative projects in the Objective 2 region of South Limburg.	1996-98
Supply chain management	RTP, Interreg (ERMN)	To form six clusters of companies in the Rhine-Meuse North Euroregion in order to develop new knowledge-intensive products and/or processes.	1996-99
Cluster project on sifting and separation methods using vacuum technology	RTP, Objective 5b	To arrive at new or innovative product-market combinations by means of cooperation on technology within the SME sector.	1997-99
Clustering Limburg Innovation Platforms (CLIP)	RTP	To facilitate a number of platforms for (technological) innovation, in which companies, knowledge institutions and intermediary organisations explore one or more themes in order to arrive at specific cooperation projects.	1997-99

The process undertaken was significant because to change the relationship between supply-based SMEs and their main customer is a costly and difficult process. The success of this particular project has given it national recognition and potential follow up through the launch of the project P* (P-Star) funded as part of the follow-up to the RTP – RIS+. The role of P* is to fill the gap where OEMs are not willing to invest in improving the technical ability of local SMEs and SMEs are unwilling to carry the financial risk involved in doing this themselves. The P* project aims to create sustainable linkages. For this reason, the objectives are for each supplier to be involved in engineering projects with several companies so that they do not become dependant on any single one, limiting the effects felt on the supplier if one of the OEMs experiences difficulties. Also, each OEM would ideally be working with four or five suppliers on separate projects. P* has not only expanded the number of OEMs and suppliers which were involved in the KIC project but also involves two other Dutch provinces. It aims eventually to become a national initiative. The philosophy is to use existing supply channels, so that it is demand, rather than supply driven: the OEMs are approached first and if they agree to participate, then their suppliers are approached, thereby avoiding the creation of artificial linkages.

Funding for implementation of the original RTP comprised various funding sources – necessary because there were no RTP specific funding sources (as shown under the project examples in Table 5.1). Those identified included the European Structural Fund Objective 2 programme of South Limburg, the Objective 5b programme for North and central Limburg and a Province programme which targets long-term industrial development and the European Fourth Framework Technology programme. The financial summary covering the 1996-97 period identified a total of 51 projects funded as part of the RTP strategy at a cost of 74.9 million Dutch guilders (€34 million). Of these, three were part of the cooperation priority (which later became the cluster element of the RTP matrix) at a cost of 1.9 million Dutch guilders (€0.9 million). Funding for the years 1998 and 1999 rose amounting to a total contribution to the RTP of 80.9 million Dutch guilders (€36.7 million) in 1998 and 108.4 million Dutch guilders (€49.2 million) in 1999 however, the contribution towards cluster development cannot be determined from these totals.

Conclusions

The cluster development approach in Limburg is, in comparison with archetypical clusters, distinctive in two ways – cluster development is part of innovation policy (as the final stage of the defined innovation process), and the clusters formed are typically on a small scale.

The relationship between cluster development and innovation policy is highlighted in the division of the innovation process into separate elements. Cluster formation as part of an innovative approach to product and process development is seen as the ultimate method of innovation for companies operating within the current economic conditions which are increasingly requiring companies to become more competitive by becoming more innovative. By working as part of an innovation cluster, existing supply chain cluster arrangements can be strengthened with a view to improving the competitiveness of the supply companies more generally and new methods of development can be explored by companies combining their various forms of expertise. The structure of viewing cluster development as part of a process allows SMEs to strive towards improving their technical base and innovation capacity to eventually become part of a cluster arrangement.

The RTP did not have a dedicated fund, so there were no distinctive funds for cluster formation. Various sources of funding were already available in the Province to support innovation but by bringing them all under one strategy, the Province managed to maximise the synergy effect of the combined funds, which offer various types of support for cluster development.

The focus of cluster formation within the RTP is on networking partnerships as a tool for improving SME skills and to create synergy. Reflecting the non-interventionist approach of the national government, the RTP not only contributes towards the creation of a suitable environment for cluster building but has measures in place which actively encourage it. No sector is targeted specifically within this framework meaning that organisations from all parts of the economy can be funded as part of a cluster arrangement so long as they are judged suitable by the implementing agencies and are willing to cooperate and innovate.

Although cluster formation to assist innovation is perceived to be beneficial to those involved, motivation to become involved in an innovation cluster very rarely comes from firms alone. A third, unrelated party or intermediary, is seen as an essential element within this process. Firms may agree that cooperation is possible but a venture of this sort can be complicated even in obtaining commitment from everyone involved. A link in the chain is usually required to work with the partners up to the point where a contract is signed. The intermediary should be familiar with the local economic structure and have good personal knowledge of local firms.

The cluster approach in the Limburg RTP supports a cluster of firms which are not direct competitors by focusing instead on vertical linkages. Supply chains, for example, work well as cluster projects because the activities of the participants are complementary – they are clearly linked in their field of activity and by joining their knowledge can create a synergy effect. In order for firms to create clusters which have value added, they have to be able to share information and technologies. For this to occur, they have to be able to offer different but compatible knowledge.

One of the RTP approaches to cluster development uses existing linkages but changes the balance of knowledge and expertise between the component supplier and OEM. The P* project uses existing supply chain linkages with the aim of improving the engineering skills of the SMEs to make them more than just producers of components. This approach was adopted because it is demand-oriented, a positive feature highlighted by research done on completion of the KIC project. This research pointed to the fact, for example, that the OEMs in the region would like suppliers with improved expertise in component design and creates more dependability between the firms involved and therefore more stability for the supplier firms.

What appears to make the cluster approach in Limburg work, is the adaptation of cluster theory to make it relevant to a theme chosen by the Province and local economic development actors – innovation – and relevant to the local area. Although the results are clustering on a small scale – micro-clusters – the tailored application uses wider cluster expertise matched with regional requirements.

Chapter 6

North-Rhine Westphalia

Peter Ache

Introduction

North-Rhine Westphalia (NRW) is a region struggling with the decline of major industries. This is particularly true in the Ruhrgebiet where new approaches to regional regeneration have been consistently explored in past decades, including the cluster approach. With regards to cluster policies, since the beginning of the 1990s, regional policy in the *Land* (state) of NRW has followed two distinctive strands. First, the policy model has shifted towards an approach characterised by scholars as 'process management' (Heinze and Voelzkow, 1991; Heinze *et al*, 1998). This focuses on the delineation of new regions with responsibility to create non-elected regional assemblies (*Regionalkonferenzen*) and develop regional strategies. Despite criticisms, this model helped to establish a more decentralised regional policy approach, based on local partnership between different public and private actors and emphasising the development of endogenous potential. Second, the *Land* defined a series of initiatives, which targeted both old industries like the automotive sector and new ones such as environmental technologies or biotechnology, with SMEs as a focus. Although this was not named a 'cluster' strategy, the initiatives were closely linked to the cluster concept.

The current approach to regional policy attempts to bring together both elements: the political and social partnership with a stronger industry orientation in the so-called 'competence economy'. Cluster ideas have taken centre stage. Indeed, NRW can be seen as an example of a region in search of a regionally integrated cluster policy. In pursuit of the 'neo-industrialisation' of under-performing industrial sectors, there is interest in both existing industrial strengths and new economic activities. While the implemented structures are still in a test phase, NRW can already look back over ten years of policies which could be classed under a 'cluster' perspective.

After a general introduction to the NRW region, subsequent chapters develop the policy background and overall approach to cluster strategies.

The focus will be on specific features of strategy development and implementation. One example of a project currently in operation in NRW is then presented before potential success factors are outlined in the conclusion.

Economic background

In 1997, the *Land* of NRW had almost 18 million inhabitants in an area covering 34,100 km², and a total employment of 7.2 million (Landesregierung NRW, 2000). In a wider German context, NRW accounted in 1996 for nearly 14 percent of the total area of the federal republic, 27 percent of its population, 26 percent of employment, 26 percent of GDP, 28 percent of exported goods and 25 percent of foreign direct investments (LDS, 1996). NRW is not only the largest *Land* in Germany, but also represents a large region in a European context.

Table 6.1: Basic economic indicators for NRW

GDP/head (PPS) EUR15=100, 1996	Employment by Sector % of total, 1997			15-64 as % of total population, 1997
	Agriculture	Industry	Services	
109.7	2.0	35.9	62.2	61.2

Source: CEC 1999b, Table 43: pp.234-35

The Ruhrgebiet is a part of the *Land* and which, together with the Dutch Randstad, forms the core of the North-Western-Metropolitan-Area (NWMA). This is a European mega-region at one stage called the 'Blue Banana' (Ache, 2001). A total of 11 million people live (1993) and 4.6 million work (1991) in the Rhine-Ruhr-agglomeration. As the name indicates, two distinctive parts of the region can be identified: the Rheinschiene (Rhine area) centred around Köln and Düsseldorf; and the Ruhrgebiet (Ruhr region) stretching from the river Rhine towards Dortmund in the east. The Ruhr region presents an example of 150-year old carboniferrous[17] capitalism which, for more than 40 years, has been in a constant state of structural change. Major parts of the Ruhrgebiet qualify under Objective 2 i.e. regions of industrial decline undergoing major structural adjustment.

A broad brush picture of the structural changes should start with the downturn of the coal and steel industries. This has impacted almost every sector and branch in the region as a result of the economy's high degree of dependency on those industries. Between 1964 and 1992, nearly 600,000 jobs were lost in industry, half of them in the mining and steel sectors. Unemployment was, and still is, a major problem in the region. Compared with the federal average of 10 percent in September 2000 (8.1 percent in West Germany) unemployment levels in NRW (9.5 percent) and the Ruhrgebiet (12.2 percent) are still very high (KVR, 2000). Sub-regional variation shows isolated areas with even higher rates – in Gelsenkirchen, for example, a city located in the centre of the Ruhrgebiet, unemployment stands at a 17.4 percent rate which is one of the highest rates in Germany, including the East German *Länder*.

More positively, the structural changes have also led to the emergence of modern structures, particularly the service economy (cf. Table 6.1). Under closer scrutiny, however, this service economy shows structural and regional weaknesses. There are only a few centres, such as Köln and Düsseldorf, which can compete in structure and quality with other, more advanced service economies in Germany (e.g. Frankfurt or München). Other parts of the region, and especially the Ruhrgebiet, do not provide these high quality, high-level services. Such areas still have a reasonable share of services, but mainly in more downstream functions which are smaller scale and less important.

The situation of Essen reflects the strong intra-regional differences in the Ruhrgebiet. Essen, which represents the core area of the region, has a relatively well-developed service economy, although still lagging behind the leading German centres. Within the Ruhrgebiet, the city of Essen is the most advanced due to the presence of the headquarters of major regional companies (Ache, 1994). The counterpart to this city are the still heavily industrialised fringes of the region, mainly in the north. These include, for example, the Emscher sub-region where coal mining and the chemical industry is concentrated, and the western parts (particularly Duisburg) which is dominated by the residual steel companies.

Regarding industries, there are also more positive developments. For example, NRW is notable as a location for international investors. In 1997, 600 firms from the US, 500 from Japan, 150 from China and 40 from Korea enriched the business environment in the Ruhr region and in NRW (LEG *et al*, 1997). However, these developments are still insufficient to bring the 'limping' Ruhrgebiet on to the same level playing field as other German regions. Overall, the economy of the Ruhrgebiet shows stable but under-performing development trends, mainly due to a handful of weak sectors and branches (Bade, 2000). The Ruhrgebiet brings down the performance indicators of NRW as a whole quite considerably.

Policy background

Since the Social Democrats have been in power in NRW, a series of structural programmes has been launched. Initially, these arouse of discussions on the need for greater economic planning in the late 1960s. As a result, an estimated budget of more than DM 46 billion (€23.5 billion) has been spent over three decades.[18]

Three phases of structural policy can be distinguished, each of which has a different approach to how the problems should be addressed (Heinze and Voelzkow, 1991).

- *Re-industrialisation* (until the end of 1970s): technology programmes were launched, aimed at the modernisation of the mining, energy and steel sectors. The common belief at that time was that the economy was merely undergoing a simple economic downturn, which would be followed by an upswing. One important infrastructure investment in that period was the establishment of the larger universities in the Ruhrgebiet, in the cities of Bochum and Dortmund.
- *Neo-industrialisation* (beginning of the 1980s): the evidence of a true structural crisis, rather than an economic downturn, became clearer at the start of the 1980s. It was clear that old industrialised structures existed which were suffering from increased international competition, substitution and market challenge. Programmes were designed to create a range of new infrastructures, a regional network of technology transfer and consulting agencies. The universities were expected to extend cooperation with industry and specific institutions, established for the region, were encouraged to coordinate locally-based projects and activities. Finally, the intention was to modernise the overall infrastructure based on the needs of modern industries, as compared to those of the carboniferrous industries.
- *Process management*: at the end of the 1980s a considerable change occurred with the introduction by the *Land* of so-called future initiatives (*Zukunftsinitiativen*). The first was *Zukunftsinitiative Montanregionen* (ZIM, future initiative for carboniferrous regions in 1987) and was designed to cope with problems resulting from the on-going changes, rather the continuing decline of mining and the large-scale changes in the steel sector. The second was *Zukunftsinitiative für die Regionen Nordrhein-Westfalen* (ZIN, future initiative for regions in NRW in 1989).

ZIM established for the first time a decentralised layer of strategy formulation, based on a SWOT (strengths, weakness, opportunities, threats) analysis of the *Montanregionen* (regions characterised by carboniferous capitalism). Following complaints from outside the Ruhrgebiet, these structures were extended throughout NRW with the introduction of ZIN. The *Land* was divided into 15 regions, each of which followed the basic organisational area of the chambers of industry and commerce. These regions were asked to set up non-elected regional assemblies *(Regionalkonferenzen)*, representing the local and county councils and various social groups of relevance to structural policy issues. A steering committee formed the organisational centre. Working groups on pre-defined topics developed basic reports which, following discussion in the assembly and the councils, were brought together into so-called regional development strategies (for an overview: Heinze and Voelzkow, 1997; Heinze *et al*, 1998).

The creation of regional development strategies was the main aim of this sub-regional political exercise. The *Land* government emphasised that the regions should set up comprehensive strategies for their future development in a self-responsible, pro-active, creative and cooperative way. Following an analysis of strengths and weaknesses, the strategies were supposed to address distinct topics such as innovation and technology, skills qualification and other labour market issues, gender questions, infrastructure, environment and energy, and other aspects, e.g. image development. These topics were provided as guidelines by the *Land* to help facilitate the process and place emphasis on certain themes. The result was supposed to be tailored to the specific strengths of the respective regions. Most of the regions have adopted a regional development strategy, but contrary to expectations, almost all the strategies were so similar that the characteristic features of the regions did not shine through and the differences were not identifiable (Ache, 1997).

The last stage of the process management phase is dominated by negotiation and cooperation processes. The key word in this context is 'partnership'. In partnership with different regional and local stakeholders, the regional development strategies try to define units which potentially offer a greater set of assets and a higher likelihood for new patterns of growth and, taking the global framework into account, therefore success in regional competition. The regional assemblies have a wide variety of participants with members coming from city councils, chambers of commerce, different professional associations, unions, voluntary organisations, churches, environmental protection groups etc. (Landesregierung NRW, 1999).

Consequently, the existing policy environment in NRW provided a strong context for the development of the cluster approach. First, there was a focus on the competitive strengths and key weaknesses of the local economy at a sub-regional level, providing the critical analysis underpinning cluster development. Second, with the use of a partnership approach in policy development, policy-making mechanisms which encompassed both public and private sector agents were already in place.

Overall cluster approach

Since 1990, cluster strategies have been discussed and gradually applied. A significant prompt in this area came through the draft Objective 2 programme in 1998-99 which defined 'clusters' as a quasi 'official policy baseline' for regional policy in NRW. The main reason for this was the preparation for the expected post-2006 changes in EU structural policy with the related aim of the *Land* government to establish 'stable', 'durable' and ultimately self-sustaining economic structures.

In the existing policy approach, critics pointed to the lack of direct targeting of economic problems and needs. The actors involved in the initial rounds of decentralised policy formulation were principally the social partners. The selection methods of these partners have, in some cases, been criticised as repeating and reinforcing the well-known corporatist structures between Social Democrat politicians (mostly the mayors), unions, carboniferrous capital and the chambers. In particular, the chambers were not considered as truly representative of regional companies because of their character as obligatory associations with almost a civil service status. The overall issue was whether the partners were capable of targeting economic needs and developing successful economic strategies. Only by the beginning of 2000 were the cluster strategies, formally introduced in the Objective 2 programme, providing this targeting of economic sectors and existing economic problems. Presented as 'competence economy',[19] the cluster approach was designed to help develop more focused regional development strategies.

The Objective 2 programme places a major emphasis on the development of the competence economy in NRW. Its importance to the strategic objectives of the programme is such that it was characterised as a horizontal aim by the *ex ante* evaluation.[20] The main development goal of the Objective 2 programme is the "creation of new and the safeguarding of existing jobs through improving the competitiveness of the region"

(Landesregierung NRW, 2000, p.207). It is divided into four sub-categories:

a.   increasing investment activities including business start-up;
b.   developing and strengthening regional competencies;
c.   improving regional infrastructures; and
d.   integrative measures.

The development of a competence economy (b), which is synonymous with cluster policy, is high up the hierarchy of goals. Business support measures are the main vehicle to implement this goal. These measures target the existing deficits in the regional economy and highlight the conceptual ideas behind the competence economy. It can do this through *general* actions particularly in the technology and innovation area. Here, the focus areas of cluster development have already been largely pre-selected by existing policy. Important competence fields are new materials, ICT, transport/logistics, energy, as well as medical and micro-system technology, new production technology (heavy engineering, machine construction), the construction sector, life sciences, design, bio and gen-technology, and environmental protection. These competence fields are not entirely new inventions of the Objective 2 Programme. On the contrary, they reflect potential strengths of the regional economy that became obvious in the course of defining regional development strategies, e.g. applying a SWOT analysis. The *Land* already provides a set of technology initiatives supporting these fields (cf.Table 6.2).

A second field of action in support of business development addresses *specific* economic competencies which exist in the region. One of which is the field of multi media and communication technologies. Multimedia technologies have been identified as a competence field, already existing in the region. The key locations for these activities are outside the designated Objective 2 region in Köln and Düsseldorf, but the *Land* hopes for spillover effects into the rest of the region. In particular, software development for the ICT sector is concentrated in the eastern part of the Ruhrgebiet in the city of Dortmund. The Objective 2 programme provides an example of how Structural Fund aims and *Land* initiatives can be integrated. The respective initiative of the *Land* is mediaNRW, which brings together key players in the sector, RTD institutes, universities and the *Land* administration. Task forces worked on topics such as telework/tele-cooperation, online services, 'electronic cities', new media and learning, multimedia/health sector and multimedia/public administration. The task forces helped identify further initiatives which are now operational at *Land* level, such as Call Centre

Offensive NRW, Electronic Commerce Offensive NRW, Initiative TeleArbeit NRW, Business TV Initiative NRW, Print and Publishing Initiative, and finally Multimedia Offensive Handwerk. The Objective 2 programme will give priority to projects relating to these initiatives.

Infrastructure development (c) also includes aspects which promote the competence economy including the support of technology and qualification institutions, service structures for logistics, and a combination of skills qualification and infrastructure development. The intention is not to establish new technology infrastructures, given the already strong supply. New technology or transfer centres will only be planned in very specific circumstances. The main objective is to develop operational links between existing RTD, universities, specialised research centres and the regional economy (with SMEs in particular). A further goal is to link such centres more closely with the skills training sector. In certain cases, e.g. the ChemSite initiative (see below), physical infrastructure development is also included.

A last aspect worth mentioning is the procedural approach outlined in the Objective 2 programme which has supported the emergence of a cluster approach. The basis approach has been undertaken in the *Land* for a number of years to positive assessment (Bachtler and Taylor, 1999). The *Land* recognises a greater need to coordinate the existing activities between different European Funds and ministries of the *Land*. The draft programme describes the competence economy as an integrating topic, where different measures (ERDF, ESF) and ministry departments cooperate closely within the same competence field. The regional assemblies and development strategies will be used to further enhance existing competencies and to integrate better the EU, *Land* and regional strategies. In particular, the regions are required to provide a more detailed definition of their existing economic profiles and outline potential clusters. In terms of the structure of the actors involved, the regional assemblies are called to extend the partnership and incorporate innovative actors or individuals. Taken together, these actions could help establish a cluster development process characterised by a strong analytical base but also trial and error and an openness for experimentation (Landesregierung NRW, 2000).

In summary, cluster policies are not entirely new to NRW. Some change has been experienced over time through the introduction of a strong technology focus, a focus on existing regional specialisms and a clearer business orientation. This has included a greater focus on the expressed needs of companies and a systematic analysis of cluster issues provided by academic debate. These changes have not significantly affected the policy approach. Indeed, the cluster strategy for the coming round is keen to further 'de-formalise' the existing approach, promoting an even more targeted but also more flexible style. The old structures e.g. regional development strategies and regional conferences will continue to exist in parallel, in particular because of their wider remit beyond purely economic issues.

The new flexible approach might take the form of a project currently conducted by a regional consultancy (ISA). As a result of experiences gained with previous 'competence economy' projects, ISA works on a 'regional policy coaching' model which trains actors on issues such as communication, process moderation, definition of aims and objectives etc. With such generic skills, they can set up and manage their own projects. This coaching is currently in a test phase and will only later potentially be offered as a service to regional actors or an even wider market.

Policy implementation

The overall picture of measures implementing the cluster or competence strategy is a complex one and includes the following elements: technology-led initiatives based on a strict cooperative approach covering the *entire Land*; local projects and initiatives; and the development of the competence economy, in particular for the Ruhr region and Objective 2 areas. The first set of initiatives goes back to the period of neo-industrialisation at the beginning of the 1980s. The second set can be linked to the period of 'process management', when the regions developed their bottom-up development strategies. The final set of initiatives, in particular the new strategy of a 'competence economy', is closely linked to the recent Objective 2 programme for the period up to 2006. Altogether, the different initiatives can be seen as a nearly 20-year period of structural policy formulation and experimentation. The 'competence economy' is synonymous for a cluster oriented approach that wants to establish an umbrella for the existing initiatives, providing at the same time a framework for new initiatives or projects.

Tables 6.2 and 6.3 provide an overview of the first category of initiatives. In all, 19 initiatives focus on specific branches and areas of technology. On closer examination, measures include:

- the establishment of technology centres (e.g. medical technology) or specific research or testing facilities (e.g. EMV, an electromagentic impact test centre);

- the promotion of new applications and the design of new products (e.g. RTD support for new materials);
- the formation of company networks (e.g. VIA, the initiative to form closer cooperation between suppliers of the automotive industries); and
- the promotion of the NRW 'competence economy' in fairs and trade exhibitions (e.g. ISEMATECH).

Table 6.2: NRW – Examples of specific initiatives

Initiative	*Focus*	*Main targets/ Cluster policy typology*
Alround e.V. (Aviation and aerospace technology)	Networking between SMEs and RTD institutes for technologically advanced projects	Emerging cluster Elements of community building
Bahntechnik (Rail technology)	Improve SME competitiveness with focus on innovation and export promotion	Mature cluster Community building and networking
Bergbautechnik (Mining technology)	Support for technology development and export	Mature cluster
Bio-Gen-Tec NRW (Bio and genetic technology)	Region specific: Rhineland *Bund/Land* programme	Emerging cluster Support networking of biotechnology companies
Chem-Site (Chem-vision) (Chemical industry)	Address locational disadvantage (pipeline) – FDI promotion	Mature cluster Networking of chemical industry
Elektromagnetische Vertraeglichkeit (Electromagnetic impact analysis)	SME focus, technology development, community building, awareness	Emerging cluster Infrastructure provision
Food Processing Initiative (Food sector)	Promotion of innovation, cooperation, logistics and quality management	Mature cluster Community building, networking
Health Care (Health care sector)	Initiative between pharmaceutical firms and unions to improve working conditions and innovation	Mature/emerging cluster Community building, networking
ISEMATECH (Measuring, sensoring)	34 companies, mainly SMEs; promotion of the industry	Mature cluster Community building, networking

Media (Media and multi media technologies)	Programme to promote multimedia application	Emerging cluster Community building
Medical Technology TZ NRW (Medical sector)	RTD, licensing, support for new investors and business start-ups	Mature/emerging cluster Technology centre Community building measures
Medizintechnik Netzwerk – MeTNet NRW (Medical technology)	About 80 SMEs in medical technology sector; information, project support, product development	Mature/emerging cluster Networking
Mikrostruktur-Initiative NRW (Micro structures and technologies)	Different measures to support and establish industry	Emerging cluster Community building and networking
Neue Materialien (New materials)	Links with medical technology and micro-system technology	Emerging cluster Community building
Tourismusverband NRW (Tourism)	Cooperation and communication in the tourism branch	Mature cluster Community building
VIA (Automotive Industry)	Networking with suppliers	Mature cluster Community building and networking
Zukunftsinitiative Textil NRW (Textile industries)	Improve cooperation in textile production, support for innovation and export	Mature cluster Networking

Eleven initiatives with cross-cutting topics complete the picture, including the following measures:

- a consensus between social partners to promote basic and further vocational training: this is a recent initiative, covering not only first qualifications for school-leavers but also the urgent need for people with computer skills;
- business start-ups in NRW: there is a strong political focus on encouraging new start-ups to combat the existing gap with other, high-performance *Länder* with a current emphasis on encouraging women and university graduates and addressing the successor problem in family businesses (mostly SMEs and ultra-small companies); and
- energy and environmental concerns.

Table 6.3: NRW – Selected cross-cutting initiatives

Initiative	*Focus*	*Main targets Cluster policy typology*
Ausbildungskonsens (Vocational training)	Social partners cooperate to improve training and qualification	Reform of vocational training
Weiterbildungsinitiative NRW (Further qualification)	Cooperation project between training providers and public institutions	Reform of vocational training
Gründungsoffensive GO (Promoting business start-ups)	Consulting and information for business start-ups	SME focus Start up from universities
Initiative Qualitätssicherung Nordrhein-Westfalen (Total quality management)	Quality management initiative addressing SME across sectors, information and communication at core	Community building
Energieagentur NRW (Energy agency)	Service provision to improve energy balance of SMEs	Awareness, communication
Landesinitiative Zukunftsenergien (Future energies)	Technology programme for new products and processes	Technology-led
Euregio (Cross-border cooperation)	EU-financed transborder cooperation for local authorities and firms	Cooperation

The lists of initiatives have been criticised in NRW (Rehfeld, Baumer and Wompel, 2000) and the extent to which the *Land* initiatives, the regional development strategies and lastly the local initiatives are interrelated must be questioned. The impression is of a parallel and non-complementary set of initiatives at the *Land* and regional and local levels. In addition to specific cluster initiatives, a number of projects targeting cooperation and network formation are also in existence – although these too are mainly uncoordinated. A comprehensive and current overview of all the initiatives or projects does not exist. Projects often end without any attempt to define the results or learn from experiences gained. The initiatives themselves are also often linked to too many programmes resulting in an unclear structure with little overview and ultimately little control.

The next section looks in more detail at one particular cluster initiative in NRW: ChemSite. This should provide a more in-depth view of the type of projects being implemented as well as the broader organisation and process of cluster initiative development in the *Land*.

ChemSite

ChemSite is a bottom-up industry initiative. The main aim is to develop an existing location for the chemical industry in the Emscher region, part of the Ruhr region. This region suffers heavily from its carboniferrous past and was already the subject of a specific initiative between 1989 and 1999, the International Building Exhibition, which tried to remedy the worst effects (Ache, 1998).

ChemSite dates back to a merger and subsequent restructuring of a major chemical production company which has operated in the region since 1938. The regional Chemische Werke Marl Huels was taken over by Degussa and both are now part of the Veba/Viag consortium within which chemical production is no longer the core business. These developments led to the introduction of the new ChemSite initiative, supported in particular by a former personnel director who was also an important political player in the region. With the existence of a core cluster of chemical industries located in the Ruhr since the 1930s and a capability for producing basic inputs into more specialised production, this initiative could be viewed as a defensive strategy. A major infrastructure development project, which targets one of the key locational disadvantages of the region, also underlines the more defensive character of the initiative (cf. Czytko, 2000).

ChemSite was initially a purely private sector project confined to a specific location. In 1997, however, it was turned into a wider regional initiative and publicly launched. The regional initiative has at its core a public-private partnership. On the private sector side, Degussa-Huels is the major industrial actor, bringing on board other companies from the chemical production chain. In terms of the public sector, the Ministry of Economic Affairs in NRW is the main player, which had defined the chemical industry as the leading sector for the entire Emscher-Lippe region. The municipalities of the Emscher-Lippe region also provide general support. The industrial union IG BCE is important for labour market questions and pay negotiations while the regional and *Land* economic development associations (ELA and GfW respectively), as well as the regional chamber of commerce and industry, provide services for incoming investors.

The essential goals of the initiative are:

- to improve the general conditions for the chemical industry;
- to encourage chemical and chemical-related companies to locate in the Emscher-Lippe region;
- to create new jobs;
- to support the establishment of innovative enterprises; and
- to attract FDI.

In particular, the initiative markets a portfolio of available locations covering a total of 640 acres across the region and concentrated at the industrial complex of Degussa-Huels at Marl. A number of companies are already in operation at the 'chemical industry park marl' (e.g. Condea, Oxeno, Bayer-Buna, Stockhausen, BP Chemicals, Vestolit, ISP), tapping into the physical material flows of Degusssa-Huels.

The organisational core of ChemSite is Infracor, a branch company of the Degussa-Huels group. Infracor is a 'one-stop service point' for the chemical industry and related services on site. It consists of three sub-projects: a location initiative, aiming at exogenous development (e.g. marketing of available/under-used sites); an alliance for innovation to support endogenous development (e.g. start-up of innovative SMEs); and ChemVision, a roundtable to discuss and initiate the further development of the entire area as a location for chemical production.

Location initiative

The main aim of the location initiative is to attract FDI to the region and strengthen its importance as a location for chemical industries. This is an 'associative' initiative between public administration, politicians and industrialists which provide a service package for potential investors. This package includes the following:

- provision of locations/sites which can be tailored to the specific requirements for raw materials, service provision/needs (laboratories, anlaytics, fire-fighters, environmental protection), transport and logistics;
- provision of highly-qualified personnel using a time-lease company;
- participation in a time-lease company on site (*Personalverbund*);
- shortened permission times for building and operation of industrial plants;
- provision of service through Infracor to obtain building permits; and

- provision of additional services including, for example, a tax base in the Netherlands to avoid high tax burdens.

This package was put together on the basis of research carried out by Infracor on the requirements of foreign investors moving into Germany. This research surveyed 200 companies to access information on needs and to market the ChemSite initiative. This research generated 40 project ideas, of which eight were realised. In terms of investment requirements, four main bottlenecks were identified which have influenced the make-up of the service package.

First, company taxation was considered too high in Germany. In order to address this, Infracor/ChemSite provides a tax-counselling model in cooperation with a major international business consultant (KPMG) designed to reduce the final tax load to a level similar to in the US. Second, labour markets were considered too rigid with low worker flexibility. Infracor, therefore, created a personnel pool at ChemSite through a time-lease company providing about 600 jobs. New trainees are regularly taken through vocational training programmes, some of whom are placed in jobs while others work through the time-lease company. The employing of trainees is advantageous for investors given their lower wage costs and the time-lease company can offer greater worker flexibility. A system of close assessment has also increased labour force discipline. Third, labour costs are considered too high. The industrial union has agreed that an overall discount of ten percent can be applied to new investors and that work councils will restrain themselves from wage demands which could damage foreign investment negotiations. Finally, foreign investors considered the regulatory framework to be overly heavy. ChemSite offers a 'certification' service for new investors to liaise and speed up the process of obtaining the required certification from the public administration. This is supported by a decision of the provincial government to accelerate administrative procedures. This service has gained a good reputation and, at present, a new investment project worth DM 1 billion (€0.5 billion) has been given entirely into the hands of the Infracor team.

Alliance for innovation

The main objective of the alliance is to stimulate business start-ups and improve the innovative performance of the region through a targeted cooperation with polytechnics, universities, technology centres and transfer agencies. The alliance is managed by a separate unit, CREAVIS (subsidiary of Degussa-Huels) and Technology Centre Marl (TechnoMarl, a local public-private partnership). Potential business start-ups are offered a range of services from business plan development to contact with venture capitalists. An important component is the cooperation with regional universities, using a business plan competition and start-up seminars for graduates from chemical science and biology in particular.

ChemVision

ChemVision is a business alliance to secure the supply of propylene, the most important raw material for local chemical companies. This is a *Land*-wide initiative which promotes the construction of a propylene pipeline connecting the region with existing networks in the Benelux area. This project is supported by the *Land* government and is one of the measures in the Objective 2 programme for 2000-06.

An advisory council coordinates the different activities of ChemSite from a strategic point of view. The council meets every quarter and Infracor is the managing office. Members of the council come from MWMEV, the decentralised government units (*Regierungspräsidenten*, regional council), GfW (economic promotion unit of the *Land*), communities (councillors, interest associations, science), partner companies of ChemSite and union representatives. A basic agreement has been signed by the council relating to activities of ChemSite. For inward investment, for example, detailed plans coordinate the activities between the ELA (a regional economic promotion unit), the advisory council, partner companies and Infracor. A number of terms and conditions have been agreed as a baseline for cooperation in the advisory council (and for ChemSite at large) including: transparency in an open marketing process (incoming investment is discussed in the entire ChemSite group); consensus between partners in case of conflicts or new ventures; and regular reports from the three sub-projects to establish a shared information basis and create better links between projects.

It is still relatively early to be able to assess the effects of the ChemSite initiative. Targeted investments to date amount to DM 200 million (€102 million) and new companies and FDI are in the pipeline. Further, despite the merger, employment appears to have stabilised. In the future, large-scale infrastructure projects may bring further investment and work to the region.

Conclusions

The final section attempts to summarise the positive and negative aspects of the competence economy and related approaches in the *Land*. The overall approach of NRW shows the following profile: the competence economy clearly follows a cluster approach with existing industries but also targets new sectors. The NRW case combines the upgrading of old and the creation of new economic activities. The competence economy has to be seen as the current stage in a history of regional development strategies – NRW has undertaken policies aimed at adjusting economic structures for more than 40 years. This history of these policy approaches has established a procedural and institutional setting on which the competence economy can build. Actors have learned lessons and know 'how to play the game', in particular how to re-invent the programme in the course of its implementation. The building blocks for an integrated cluster strategy can be found in the regional development strategies, comprising a number of regional development models. NRW also links the competence economy into its EU programmes (especially Objective 2). As a final point, the *Land* government also has ideas about certain clusters, illustrated by the technology-led initiatives.

The situation in NRW has certain highly specific characteristics in comparison to the other case-study regions. NRW is a very large region which, in economic terms, is equivalent to countries such as the Netherlands or Denmark. This naturally provides a different starting point for regional or industrial policy. NRW still has a strong industrial basis, despite the under-performance in terms of growth and the decline of key sectors. It is a huge regional economy, or set of sub-regional economies, with a wide range of sectors. The regional economy provides a whole series of inter-related points for cluster-like developments and the stimulus of new economic activities. The problematic region is the Ruhrgebiet with its dominant old industrial structures. NRW has a well established technology/transfer, RTD and university institutional background which can stimulate technological change (and provides qualified personnel).

The positive components of the cluster and competence economy approach include: the mixture of old and new industries, which are targeted by the strategy; the procedural dimension that is characterised by strong background analysis but also trial-and-error and openness, regarding target sectors and clusters in particular; and the policy consultation and policy development process, with a number of academic institutes actively integrated into the development of the strategy. This has partly led to a confusing number of programmes and initiatives, often weakly integrated together. However, while the overall landscape remains complex, with overlap and lack of coordination, the Objective 2 programme is starting to remedy this situation.

A separate point, which needs to be addressed here is the 'stamina' of NRW regional policy. This is a heavily debated feature of structural policy in NRW, in particular regarding the financial resources which have been pumped into the structures. This is considered to have led to a negative 'structural' policy, which has mixed sectoral policies effectively conserving industrial structures with a regional policy aimed at the creation of new activities (Hamm and Wienert, 1990). Some observers have suggested that money should be spent entirely on new industries.

Overall, NRW illustrates the case of both a defensive and pro-active cluster strategy. There is a combination of both mature and emerging cluster initiatives and a number of the local cases might also be characterised as 'wishful thinking' clusters. The measures to implement the competence economy bring together elements of community building (identifying potential clusters, but mainly in the course of regional strategy formulation), networking of specific companies (especially under the umbrella of technology led initiatives and the more closely defined industry clusters), and finally provision of common resources (with a small number of infrastructure projects in particular).

NRW has almost 20 years of experience with different cluster-related initiatives, but cluster thinking and related projects are still effectively in their development stage. The main results to emerge from this approach will only be seen in the future. The Objective 2 programme may be very important in this regard. Clusters here are viewed as a horizontal goal, integrating different existing programmes and initiatives, sectoral and regional policies as well as coordinating different administrative structures. This characterises the strategy and policy-making process as one not only supported by strong analysis but also open to trial and error, particularly with regard to target sectors and cluster development.

Notes

[17] A neologism deliberately created to point to the two most important components in the industrial development of the region: coal (carbon) and steel (ferro). Börner (2000) provides a comprehensive and recent overview on the Ruhr region in this context.

[18] This does not include initiatives of other ministries (mainly the Ministry for Labour, Health, Social Matters, MAGS). More recently, the intention has been to coordinate the different activities more closely. EU funds account for 60 percent

of the current budgets available for regional policy (Landesregierung NRW, 1999, p.44).

[19] The rephrasing of clusters as 'competence economy' reflects the path of the political debate in NRW. One key event is considered to have been a paper provided by the SPD suggesting that cluster policy be given an official status. This resulted in critical comments from the Christian Democrat party and chambers of commerce, in particular. Both feared *Investitionslenkung*, the control of industrial investment by way of focusing all policy efforts on specific clusters. The terminology of competence economy was then introduced, seemingly a less challenging concept to the critical parties. On the other hand, an early draft of the O2 Programme, suggesting that a cluster approach be explicitly followed, has also resulted in harsh comments from the chambers.

[20] The *ex ante* evaluation is required by EU ERDF guidelines. This evaluation has been provided by *MR Regionalberatung (Delmenhorst), InWis – Institut für Wohnungswesen und Immobilienwirtschaft, Stadt- und Regionalentwicklung (Bochum)*, and *Netherlands Economic Institute* (NEI, Rotterdam).

Chapter 7

País Vasco

Sandra Taylor

Introduction

Of the territories examined in this volume, País Vasco has been one of the most active and pioneering in pursuing cluster development. The Basque Government embraced the cluster approach enthusiastically in the early 1990s with a full-scale cluster mapping exercise and a separate policy to develop clusters in its major industrial competences, a policy which it has continued to pursue since. Over time, cluster development has not only been subject to its own set of policy actions, but the concept has been incorporated into the territory's industrial development strategies as both an organising principle and a criteria for business support. It should also be seen as part of a longer tradition of País Vasco developing more systemic approaches to revitalising its industry. Active support for business innovation and its integration into regional economic development has long characterised the territory's approach to reversing industrial decline which is distinctive in a Spanish context (Tödtling and Kaufmann, 2000).

As the following chapter details, another distinguishing feature of Basque cluster policy is the substantial involvement of the private sector in the design and delivery of policy. Elements of the cluster policy – notably cluster selection and policy implementation – have been transferred to cluster representatives within the private sector through the designation of a coordinating organisation for each cluster and the structuring of some cluster activities through multi-annual strategic agreements (*convenios*) signed between those organisations and the Basque government. Unlike some of the regions in the book, the role of public sector in País Vasco has been more clearly one of a 'facilitator' than an 'animateur'.

Economic background

País Vasco has a population of just over two million inhabitants. In contrast with most other parts of Spain, it has been characterised by a long history of industrialisation (alongside the Madrid region and Cataluña). It also has a dense tissue of SMEs. In parallel with economic factors, the political, constitutional and geographical context of País Vasco have been important determinants of the development of industrial policy. This is reflected in the region's policy autonomy. Spain is an asymmetric federal state. Under negotiated agreements, País Vasco has delegated responsibility for many policy fields which, in other regions, are managed nationally. Among them is economic development policy.

The Basque economy was dominated by foundry and shipbuilding industries until the 1970s when both sectors saw drastic decline in the face of competition from elsewhere. Following this collapse, there was a perceived need to modernise and reorient the Basque productive structure. This was given further impetus in the early 1990s, when a renewed period of recession had a significant impact on the regional economy. To date, although it continues to hold an important position in the Spanish economy, particularly in terms of GDP per capita and exports, the region has high unemployment (especially among low-skilled workers) compounded by a number of characteristics of local companies which limit their capacity to innovate.

Industrial activity has long represented a significant proportion of the Basque economy. In 1985, while roughly half of all employment in Spain and in the Basque country was in the service sector, 38 percent of Basque employment was in industry, compared to just 24 percent across Spain as a whole. Over time, the relative dominance of industry has declined in the Basque country while services have grown (the balance in 1995 being 29 percent versus 60 percent). The increasing tertiarisation of the Basque economy has taken place relatively slowly and been linked to increasing employment associated with the regional government and growth in services to industry. The relative importance of industrial employment led economic regeneration policies in the late 1980s to focus on the regeneration of this sector rather than promoting employment creation through tertiarisation, which was considered to present limited prospects.

In terms of the weight of specific sectors in the Basque economy, commerce, metal-related industries and business services are among the largest employers and contributors to the regional product. However, the distinguishing feature of the regional economy is its diversity, with a spread of employment across a wide range of activities. The list of clusters supported in País Vasco provides a useful indication of what are perceived to be the most significant current or future sectors in the region. For example, the automotive sector consists of 249 companies in País Vasco (out of 650 for Spain as a whole), representing 34 percent of Spanish automotive turnover. Other key activities include tool making, white goods, and environment-related industries, notably waste processing.

Origins of the cluster approach

The formal catalyst for Basque cluster policy was the commissioning of a study on Basque sources of competitive advantage by the Monitor consultancy in 1990, making the territory one of the first in Europe to actively embrace Michael Porter's cluster-based ideas. To understand why the cluster approach was adopted though, it is necessary to appreciate the longer-term context for economic development policy-making in País Vasco.

As a regional authority, the Basque Government has had a highly active role in economic development policy deriving from its extensive negotiated policy and tax rights as a *Comunidad Autónoma* within the Spanish state. In addition to the *Diputaciones Forales* (an intermediate tier of sub-regional government), the regional level retains most of its collected revenue (including income tax) for use in a wide range of policy areas over which it has autonomy, including economic development policy.

The impetus for cluster policy in País Vasco has come almost entirely from the regional level, unsurprisingly since responsibility for economic development policy has been delegated to this tier from the national level. The leading proponent has been the government of the *Comunidad Autonoma del País Vasco* (specifically the Competitiveness unit within of the Department of Industry, Commerce and Tourism), although a range of other regional and sub-regional actors have also been involved.

The Basque Country in the early 1990s provided a favourable context for the introduction of cluster policies for several reasons. First, the regional government had both the scope and the desire to innovate to benefit the regional economy: it had recently gained extended economic development powers, and wished to take the initiative to stem the economic decline caused by the collapse of traditional industrial sectors and counter the threats posed by increasing globalisation. The Government was receptive to new ideas and looked outside Spain for theories and approaches which were capturing the international imagination.

Second, the pre-requisites for the cluster approach were satisfied in terms of the regional business population: there was a dense population of locally-owned SMEs in diverse industrial sectors, with business traditions focused on cooperation and informal networks. The region has a long history of industrial association and networking, as well as a notable record of spin-offs. A large number of cooperative firms exist, for the most part, geographically concentrated in the valleys of Guipúzkoa, the best known of these being Mondragón (Aranzadi, 1999).

Third, the potential of cluster policy to strengthen indigenous firms by increasing their interactions was appealing because of the pervasive socio-political desire for regional self-reliance, driven by a strong sense of Basque identity. País Vasco is a relatively small region, whose sense of identity has been reinforced by its distinctive linguistic and cultural traditions and its considerable political autonomy. This cohesiveness may have facilitated the establishment of cluster policy by the Basque Government. It also provided an alternative to relying on inward investment, an economic development objective of many other Spanish regions. Violent Basque separatist activity may have been a deterrent to foreign investment in the region, and this may in turn have reinforced the Government's choice of an economic development strategy strongly oriented towards self reliance.

Finally, there were also already policy precedents which, while they were not the direct catalysts for cluster policy, had prepared the way for these ideas. In particular, there had been a strong emphasis on applied technology policy in the region, continuing since the mid-1980s, and an associative approach to delivering selected business support policies (e.g. designing and delivering joint training initiatives for groups of firms).

The evolution of cluster policy to date can be divided into two phases. The first, delimited by the 1991-95 Basque Competitiveness Plan, was the establishment of the policy, which involved initiating the structures and strategies shaping clusters and beginning to change behaviours and perceptions. The second stage, between 1996 and 1999, entailed Basque industrial policy supporting the embedding and consolidation of the clusters.

Currently, 11 Basque clusters are the explicit subject of cluster policy: some are clearly sector-based (e.g. automotives, ICT), while others have a more horizontal, cross-sectoral dimension (e.g. 'knowledge', energy). Their selection has been a progressive and extended process (Table 7.1) with distinct roles played by the public and private sectors. For each cluster, a coordinator has been designated to take the lead in implementing the policy: coordinators have all been drawn from the private sector, where possible drawing on existing industry-based associations.

Table 7.1: Timetable of cluster formation in País Vasco

Date	*Cluster*	*Coordinator*	*Newly created?*
1992	Electrical appliances	ACEDE	Yes
	Machine tools	AFM	No
1993	Automotive	ACICAE	Yes
1994	Port	UNIPORT	No
	ICT	GAIA	No
1995	Environment	ACLIMA	Yes
1996	'Knowledge'	Cluster Conocimiento	Yes
	Energy	Cluster de Energía	Yes
1997	Aeronautics	HEGAN	Yes
1998	Paper	CLUSPAP	Yes
2000	Shipping and Marine Industries	ADIMDE	Yes

The choice of clusters involved a mixture of public sector direction and private sector confirmation. Initial proposals for priority clusters were made in the public sector-commissioned Monitor study. The study suggested targeting six sectors for development: machine tools; white goods; high value-added steel; forestry; leisure and travel; and Rioja wine (Monitor, 1991). This shortlist was reached through an analysis of regional business activity, moderated by the authors according to whether different sectors required and/or were believed likely to benefit from policy input. Some sectors were omitted as they were already well established, or not considered significant or promising. The final list did not wholly reflect the perceived economic strengths as viewed by the region's institutions and firms, in part because of the criteria used to define strengths, for example, with a strong focus on export performance, and in part because of the reliance of analysis on industrial classification systems which obscured some cluster patterns. In particular, the automotive components sector was a key omission, neglected as firms were classified under the materials they processed, not the end product to which they contributed.

The study's sponsors in the regional government accepted the principles of the recommendations, including the emphasis on using associative means to increase the competitiveness of the region's SMEs and combat the threats posed by accelerating globalisation and increasing international competition. However, a dialogue was launched to adjust the list of potential clusters to better reflect regional perceptions and priorities. Machine tools, white goods and steel were retained from the Monitor list, and supplemented by: paper, aeronautics, automotives, environment, the Port of Bilbao, business knowledge, telecommunications, and energy.

The Basque Government provided a standard methodology for the selected industrial groups to take the cluster idea forward (developed with Monitor), but it was left to the private sector to decide whether or not to do this. Not all potential clusters took up the invitation. Determining factors included the situation of each cluster (stability appeared to be a key condition for taking on a developmental commitment) and the willingness of relevant firms to dedicate personnel and resources to the initiative and to contribute financially to the policy. Where potential participants were unwilling to take up the initiative, a cluster was not launched. This emphasis on passing responsibility early to the private sector (although they have had relatively little influence at the identification phase) was critical. It was believed that if relevant industrial groups were not committed, then the policy had no business foundation and should be abandoned.

However, it appears likely that firms in reality made their decision based not only on business imperatives, but also on the impact of their choice on the future availability of public sector business support. Much future funding for business development was to be awarded preferentially to firms participating in clusters. In addition, future public RTD expenditure would also be articulated through clusters (as discussed in more detail below), so firms were more likely to have influence and benefit if they acted together to define their priorities. Finally, there was a strong socio-political (loyalty-based) imperative to adopt the idea in that the Basque Government was perceived to be taking the initiative to support Basque industry where the national government had failed to step in.

For each cluster which came forward, the methodology to be applied involved the establishment of a multi-sectoral Working Group which had to work systematically using a common methodology to address three tasks:

- *to identify options* using a detailed analysis of the cluster's current competitive strengths and weaknesses in an international context, and then to prioritise between them;
- *to define a plan of action* to realise the priorities identified, distinguishing actions to be undertaken by individual firms, groups of firms and the public sector (including the definition of ways to evaluate and control the plans and contingency plans in case the sector evolved differently than was anticipated); and
- *to launch implementation.*

Each Working Group operated with the support of consultant facilitators, and included representatives of relevant firms, the Basque Government, and education, training and basic and applied research organisations. Each was chaired by a president drawn from one of the firms in the cluster, who was selected by the regional government and the firms involved, on the basis of their sound business background, considerable standing among the business community and appropriate personal qualities including dynamism, a practical approach and international experience. The main Working Group for each cluster was subsequently supplemented by further Working Groups to address specific issues. The Basque Government proposed three groups, addressing RTD, internationalisation and quality/human resource development, with clusters free to establish further groups as appropriate. The Working Groups and their sub-groups have continued to operate, supporting and structuring the work of their cluster on an ongoing basis, and involving individuals with appropriate experience from partner firms.

The outcome of the initial Working Groups was to develop general strategic plans which were then discussed with the Basque Department of Industry. The plans summarised the aims and tasks of each cluster, setting out specific structured objectives linked to monitoring indicators. Following negotiation with the regional government, these plans became a form of contractual agreement, or *convenio,* signed between the cluster and the Government. Public sector resources have been committed to the *convenios* and their proposed activities, with subsidies of up to 70 percent for a variety of activities, many of which have been funded through mainstream economic development policies.

Over time, further clusters have either taken up the invitation to form which at first was declined (such as paper) or proposed themselves for consideration. The regional government has welcomed new clusters taking the initiative, where they can make a sufficient case. For example, the information and communication technologies sector was initially omitted by the Basque Government because it was believed that its active, existing professional association made policy intervention unnecessary. This view changed as it became clear how important ICTs would be to overall regional economic competitiveness, resulting in the sector becoming the target of cluster policy by 1993.

Overall, the cost implications to the regional government have been limited, and this responsiveness makes the policy firmly private sector led and ensures it is inclusive, where it could otherwise be seen as unfairly favouring selected firms. Although not driven by saving money, cluster policy has been relatively inexpensive for the Basque Government. The main cluster-specific expenditure has been co-financing the cluster co-ordination structures. Supporting the cluster associations costs some 300 million pesetas (€2 million) per year for the 11 clusters now existing. The cost could be considered even lower in that these structures help to make other, previously existing, areas of expenditure more effective, including training and RTD plans. The key aim of the policy is to change mentalities, by altering the way businesses work with each other and the way they view their environment. Structures pursuing this type of goal can be inexpensive to establish and run, especially if their aim is to encourage others into action rather than undertake initiatives themselves.

Otherwise, the Basque Government has continued broadly with the business development policies it operated previously, although with an adjusted focus. First, firms are actively encouraged to participate in policies as groups. Second, the additional intelligence generated by encouraging firms to interact and express the priorities of their cluster has been used to improve the relevance of economic development interventions more generally. This is most clearly seen in support for applied technological development policy. Expenditure on applied technology policy is informed by multi-annual plans developed by clusters including aeronautics, automotives, energy, environment, ICT, 'knowledge', machine tools, and white goods. To develop the plans, cluster-based Technological Development Committees meet bringing together firms (which tend to have short-term and company-specific priorities) and RTD organisations, including technology centres (which can introduce a longer term and more strategic dimension to discussion). The Committees meet to agree research priorities across a defined future timeframe, then this information is submitted to the Basque Government, which uses it to inform its own overall technology programme, attached to allocated funding. Generally, it is understood that a proposal which is linked with a cluster plan is more likely to be prioritised for public funding than a stand-alone proposal.

The cluster approach in practice

The Basque clusters are operationalised through a relatively standard range of basic elements. They are each steered by their Working Groups, described above, whose members represent the interests of the wider cluster. They each have a core membership of not only private firms, but also associate technology centres and training/educational institutions as partners with special expert status. Lastly, they are overseen by specialised coordinating organisations, set up to embody the cluster and articulate policy in collaboration with the Basque Government.

Every cluster has a designated cluster coordinator. These were not a predetermined element, but instead arose from the findings of the initial cluster Working Groups which concluded independently that, while the private sector had a key role to play, it could only achieve this with the support of a coordination body with the resources to take recommendations forward actively and represent the wider body both to cluster members and externally. The aim of cluster associations is to become directly involved with their sector, acting on behalf of their constituent firms by looking for business opportunities, building up a cluster profile for marketing, etc. They ensure their clusters have a strong presence internationally through trade missions and conference participation and act as catalysts in facilitating information exchange and interaction. The structures are non-profit making private organisations, funded by the Basque Government, membership fees from firms in the cluster, and payments for services provided to the cluster.

All cluster coordinating groups have an obligation to provide services and benefits for the *whole* cluster and not just those companies which pay for their services or for membership – otherwise, they would be mere industry associations (although some coordinators originated as this type of association). The risk here is that, without such strictures, the coordinating bodies would simply grow into standard sector associations, and respond to their own momentum rather than serving and facilitating a wider group. In theory, once the linkages are sufficiently active in a cluster, the cluster associations should no longer be needed.

The clusters vary in terms of the breadth of firms actively involved. The breadth of scope was determined by the groups of firms themselves, rather than being an externally driven outcome. There was no initial clear idea about how broad each cluster should be, so they defined themselves from within, depending on the situation of the sector and the firms which got involved. Historical factors had considerable influence. For example, machine tools was traditionally a cohesive sector and was already clearly delimited to its participants. There was a lot of cooperation even before the cluster concept was introduced, with good relations, habits of joint working and the existence of a formal machine tools association (which became the cluster association, AFM). Other sectors have been more difficult to define, such as environment. This cluster is diverse, but dominated by waste treatment businesses which grew because of the high local density of polluting industries. The composition of the cluster is not immediately apparent from its name (ACLIMA), its promotional materials or its stated aim. However, the dominant firms influence how the cluster works and its priorities.

In terms of the membership of clusters, there have been several approaches taken: to offer the same grade of membership and the same rights to all firms wishing to join; to provide different levels of formal membership, at different costs; and to limit formal membership to a sub-group of firms deemed most able to make an active contribution. This last approach has been used in the automotive cluster (ACICAE) and arose because it had no history of association. It was felt that actively involving too many firms in the early stages would lead to passivity among the members and that the necessary inter-connections and dynamics would not form. With a smaller but slowly growing group of formal, active members, it is hoped that a stronger, deeper dynamic of community building will take place. Eventually, all firms would be members. In spite of this argument, the cluster's approach has been disputed by the regional government which would like to see all clusters involve all their constituent firms, insofar as this is possible.

Although working under a common framework, each cluster is being developed through its own distinct strategy. As described above, these strategies are developed by cluster-specific Working Groups, modified and agreed in dialogue with the regional government, then delivered and monitored with the support of the cluster coordination organisations.

In each cluster, a wide range of activities has been undertaken, primarily addressing the following four areas:

- *entity building*: initial establishment of the cluster and reinforcing its identity and image externally;
- *community building*: encouraging an increased frequency and depth of interactions between the members of a cluster, increasing members' knowledge about and understanding of their cluster and engendering a sense of ownership/common interest, making the cluster 'come alive';
- *project/linkage building*: where specific projects or concrete long-term associations arise from the existence of the cluster and its interactions; and
- *externalities*: the provision of common services by/to the cluster (which firms individually would not procure) which facilitate improvements in the sector's economic performance by enhancing the performance of individual firms.

Examples of measures implemented by each of the cluster coordinators are provided in Table 7.2. In a process of ongoing reporting and monitoring, each cluster coordinating organisation submits a report to the cluster members and the regional government at six monthly intervals, summarising expenditure and the cluster's activity towards implementing its strategy. The focus, however, is arguably more on how the cluster has performed economically, and what role the cluster strategy has played in this, rather than on how the clusters have developed as entities in themselves.

Table 7.2: Examples of measures in País Vasco clusters

Activity	Example
Entity building	
Designating cluster coordinator	All Basque clusters
Cluster visibility	'Brand' development, using websites, joint materials etc.
Promoting cluster abroad	Cluster de Energia: through visits and projects
	Cluster Conocimiento: international congress
Community building	
Strategy building	All clusters produce development strategies
Increasing contact between participants	Regular meetings of cluster Working Groups
Increased communication between participants	Use of websites
Project/linkage building	
Fora for firms with specific characteristics	Cluster Conocimiento: firms with advanced management systems meet together
	Cluster de Energía: creating an organisation specialising in coordinating underground infrastructure works
Encouraging internationalisation	ACICAE (automotives)
Promoting participation in European programmes	GAIA for ICT-related initiatives
Cooperation between firms/technology centres	ACLIMA (environment), HEGAN, ACICAE

Externalities	
Promoting specific activities beneficial to cluster firms	GAIA: promoting teleworking, electronic commerce and multimedia
	HEGAN: establishing uniform quality standards
Developing training plans	Cluster de Energia, GAIA
Brands for sub-groups	GAIA: creating a brand label for Basque software
Training events	Cluster Conocimiento: international management trends
	Cluster de Energía: energy saving
Facilitating procurement from within the cluster	HEGAN, ACLIMA
	CLUSPAP (paper): sales consortium.
Lobbying on common issues of concern to the cluster	ACLIMA
Generating knowledge to better focus Basque Government strategy	Close liaison between Basque clusters and public sector
	Each cluster has a technology committee to identify future research priorities and feed back into the regional industrial policy
Providing information: new business databases	Cluster Conocimiento: register of consultancy firms
	ACLIMA: information point accessed on intranet
Providing information: access to existing databases	Cluster de Energia: providing access to EU and UN databases
Trade missions	GAIA

Several of the clusters are distinctive in that the services they provide and the activities they undertake can be horizontal, benefiting other service and manufacturing sectors, and, indeed, other clusters. The potential horizontal role of selected clusters – notably knowledge, ICT, energy and, to a lesser extent, environment – has been difficult to bring about. Clusters with this potential are still looking for a strong role among the other clusters.

To illustrate the operations of clusters in more detail, examples of cluster coordinating bodies are discussed below: ACICAE, which oversees the automotives cluster; and GAIA, responsible for ICT.

Clusters in practice: ACICAE

Automotives is a mature sector in País Vasco, although with emerging high-tech strengths in some areas. The sector is very significant to the region, accounting for some 40 percent of the total Spanish automotive industry. Around 260 suppliers are part of the region's automotive cluster, producing a wide variety of components, including engine parts, brakes, gear boxes, etc. Also associated are raw materials and capital good suppliers, and, at the other end of the chain, car makers.

The cluster coordinator, ACICAE, was created by 12 companies in 1993, with the aim of improving the competitiveness of the Basque automotive cluster by grouping leading companies together, carrying out inter-company activities and coordinating activities with car makers. The structure also explicitly aimed to work with the Basque administration and technology suppliers in País Vasco. While there are 200-300 firms in the sector, only 27 are now formally members of the cluster coordination association, although the structure has a clear vocation to serve the whole sector in the region. The wider group receive information and opportunities, but are more loosely involved. The limited membership was a strategic decision to ensure that the structure grew gradually and created a firm foundation. This was believed to be preferable to trying to introduce a network dynamic to a large group unused to working together.

The automotive cluster's members were selected from firms whose products are directly used in vehicle production, but who also have a strong local affiliation. As such, the main car manufacturer represented in País Vasco is excluded from formal membership because, being a multinational, its decisions are not made locally. It was not sufficiently embedded in the local economy to earn a decisive role in the automotive cluster. Firms like this are associated with the cluster and can participate fully, but would not be members. This contrasts with the aeronautic cluster, which has a single large aeronautic firm at its core.

Clusters in practice: GAIA

As noted above, the telecommunications sector was not at first made a priority for cluster development because there was already a sectoral association for telecommunications firms. However, three things led to a change of direction: first, lessons from developing the other clusters indicated that cluster coordinators were distinct from sectoral organisations (not only in their focus but also in involving not just producers of services but also their users); second, ICT was rapidly becoming more important to the Basque economy; and third, there was a perceived need for a structure which would help to mobilise common RTD projects to the benefit of both suppliers and users.

Arthur Andersen facilitated the development of the ICT cluster strategy in 1995, helping to elaborate options and prioritise between them. Preparatory work included compiling an overview of international trends in the ICT sector and an analysis of the competitive positioning of País Vasco (including the quality of infrastructure, the quality of support organisations and demand factors). Once overall strategic aims were decided, the concrete measures to achieve them were established. It was decided that since the Basque telecommunications industry association already undertook 80 percent of the activities of a cluster coordination organisation, it should take on this role for the new cluster. Consequently, in 1996, this organisation was transformed into one called GAIA, with a broader focus, membership and remit, to fully embrace ICT and cluster promotion issues.

GAIA moved from having 33 members in its former incarnation to having the participation of 147 companies. New members move into a context where behaviours, relationships and systems are well established, bringing a certain stability to the structure as it grows. This echoes ACICAE's membership choices. Similarly, in establishing the cluster, care was taken not to give large firms too much influence. To do this, limits were set, for example, preventing any single group from having more than two representatives active in the cluster or on a committee at the same time.

Conclusions

Clusters have been an intuitively appealing solution to economic development in the Basque Country. The severe decline which had taken place in Basque industry may have meant that people were particularly willing to adopt the cluster idea. However, it also coincided with both internal characteristics (notably traditions of business cooperation and a strong desire for self-determination) and external drivers. The external drivers were the increasing emphasis on proximity and cultural factors in determining regional business success, and the need to find new mechanisms to compete in an increasingly globalised economy.

These factors, combined with the autonomy of policy-making at regional level, the perceived need to fill a vacuum left by national level policy-making and the inaccessibility of more traditional economic development policy instruments (such as the attraction of inward investment) all combined to make the cluster approach a highly attractive policy option. In essence, País Vasco demonstrates what could be called an 'anti-bandwagoning' effect in the pursuit of cluster development.

Cluster policy received strong and early support from relevant interests. Those leading industrial policy in the 1980s and 1990s in the Basque Government – a newly created institution exploring the limits of its policy responsibilities – were drawn from both industry and research. As such, they had very different priorities, knowledge and contacts than they would have had with long-running public administration careers. This has undoubtedly affected the approaches taken in País Vasco, including the strong emphasis placed on non-interventionist business development, placing the initiative with firms themselves to shape their environment and to guide the public sector in its interventions. Those proposing cluster policy in the regional government also had strong political support among industrialists, which may have helped the policy to become more quickly embedded.

At the same time, there was also a perceived need for the public sector to be 'near to firms' – to place them at the centre of policy and be responsive to their needs. The Basque Government has made significant efforts to create this environment. The policy process has become more involved as a result, with increased consultation and strategy building activity. It would be simpler for the Basque Government to take decisions on economic development without consulting or building in the cluster structures, but they believe their interventions are more relevant and thus more effective because these structures bring them real business intelligence and approval.

Arboníes (1997) believes that – at least in the context of the Cluster Conocimiento – the initial activities of the network were important in increasing visibility, developing a sense of belonging and facilitating communication. This stage would be less important where a group of firms already had sectoral associations and/or thought of themselves as having connections and identity – but for many of the clusters, this was not the case. Cluster policy has had an important effect in creating communal self-awareness among firms. The process can be likened to viewing 'Magic Eye' pictures – assisting observers in seeing something previously hidden in a wider landscape but which had always in fact been there.

To date, cluster policy has been pursued through the elaboration and agreement of three rounds of multi-annual plans. There has been a clear evolution of the policy over time, but it is seen more as an ongoing commitment which is kept under review than as one with clear pre-agreed trigger points for public sector withdrawal (although the regional government always intended that, over time, the public contribution to the cluster coordination bodies themselves would be phased out, as the clusters became so dynamic that they could propel themselves forward). A formal 'exit strategy' was not set out in advance by the public sector for cluster policy, with a defined timetable and targets, nor has there been a clear prior expectation of how the clusters would develop and what role the public sector should have at each stage. Instead, the regional government has taken a responsive approach, taking stock at regular intervals and adjusting policy accordingly.

However, for as long as the cluster coordinators exist, there is little urgency for the public sector to withdraw for two reasons. First, the intelligence provided by the clusters is believed to enable improved targeting of relevant public sector economic development funding – a reward which offsets the cost of subsidising the cluster coordinators. Second, the continuing public sector financial input to these organisations ensures that the regional government has influence over how they are structured and operated. They can impose restrictions on their size and activities (ensuring that they continue to facilitate the activities of others rather than growing as organisations in their own right) and verify that all firms in a cluster, not just key members, are included and can benefit. Cluster coordinators are considered to have a distinct role and remit to that of sectoral associations, but there is a real danger of them slipping into the latter role (doing rather than facilitating, and involving individual members rather than the wider constituency). This may be more straightforward but is considered less relevant to cluster objectives.

Chapter 8

Scotland

Philip Raines

Introduction

The Scottish experience of cluster development policy is one of the most famous in Europe. Although it has been fully implemented only recently, the cluster approach adopted by the territory's regional development body, Scottish Enterprise, has already been the model for other areas developing their own policy, most notably, the English regions. As a highly visible example of a cluster policy, the Scottish approach combines a sense of departure from existing policy traditions with a comprehensive, strategic application of the concept to all stages of the policy-making process. The agency has been systematic in interpreting the policy implications of the cluster concept, in terms of its use in analysing the economy, its impact on the agency's own organisation, the importance of partnership in developing and implementing the policy, and its plans for monitoring and evaluating the effects. In scale terms alone, the resources dedicated to cluster development make it distinctive compared to many of the other case studies in this volume.

Despite the considerable fanfare surrounding the policy, questions remain over how far the cluster approach has led to a permanent reorientation of economic development policy in Scotland. The programmes which have been introduced have a fixed duration and remain self-contained within Scottish Enterprise. As a result, to understand the real importance of the cluster approach in Scotland, it is necessary to look beyond the specific details of the cluster programmes and consider how cluster concepts have informed the wider policy-making community.

Economic background

Up until recently, the Scottish economy had been marked by a prolonged period of industrial decline. Before 1990, Scotland had per capita income significantly below, and unemployment rates above, UK averages (Scottish

Office, 1991). Scotland divides into a series of sub-regional economies, each of which has been weakened by distinctive deep-seated structural problems. As a result of greater global competition in its core industries, the Central Belt area – framed by the urban agglomerations of Glasgow and Edinburgh – suffered from several decades of contraction in traditional manufacturing, notably shipbuilding, iron and steel production, and coal mining. The nature of the area's industries meant that Scotland's enterprise structure was historically skewed towards large firms, with the attendant risk of dependence on the fortunes of individual companies. Decline within a traditional economic activity also affected the southern, more rural areas of the Borders and the South West (in this case, textiles and clothing). By contrast, the northern part of Scotland – the Highlands and Islands – has been characterised by underdevelopment, dependence on rural activities and peripherality (in terms of low population densities and large distances to key markets).

Nevertheless, much of Scottish industry has experienced revival over the last few decades (Stories and Horne, 1999). Local pockets of industrial growth have emerged, most notably the concentration of oil and gas activity in the Grampian area, taking advantage of North Sea resources. A gradual shift in Scottish economic development strategy, following the increasing transfer of policy autonomy to regional-level agencies (particularly the Scottish Development Agency, and its successor, Scottish Enterprise), has also been partly responsible for new areas of growth. This is perhaps most visible in the territory's successful inward investment promotion strategy, resulting in a concentration of foreign-owned producers and local suppliers in the electronics industry. Based largely in the Central Belt (the so-called 'Silicon Glen'), electronics investment has made Scotland the leading production area for PCs and one of the main sources of semiconductors manufacturing in Europe. Over half of employment in the sector is accounted for by foreign employers. Moreover, foreign investment has had a key part in expanding and deepening the Scottish export base over the last two decades, as many of the foreign-owned plants are heavily export-oriented (Raines, Turok and Brown, 2001).

As a result, Scotland's economic strengths are a mixture of persistent traditional activities and emerging areas of competitive advantage. In manufacturing, this can be seen by examining the two main sectors by employment – electrical engineering/electronics and food/drink – which have also been given a high profile within Scottish Enterprise's cluster strategy.

Electronics and related industries have been one of the principal engines for recent economic growth in Scotland, responsible for the overall growth in total industrial output and increasing exports relative to the UK as a whole (Scottish Executive, 2000a). Output in Scotland's electronics industry grew by an average of over 20 percent each year between 1992 and 1996 and employment increased to over 40,000 in the industry directly, with an estimated additional 30,000 in supplier businesses (Scottish Enterprise, 1999). Electronics increased its share of total Scottish manufacturing employment from under 10 percent in 1992 to nearly 13 percent in 1995. By 1995, investment (as defined as net capital expenditure by the electronics industry) accounted for 40 percent of all investment by Scottish manufacturing industries.

Nevertheless, while electronics has continued to grow as a sector, concerns have been expressed by how much *Scottish* companies have been able to realise the benefits, especially suppliers to the foreign-owned original equipment manufacturers. Recent surveys of procurement by the largest foreign electronics companies in Scotland have shown that the share of purchases directed to Scottish firms actually declined from 20 to 17 percent in 1995 (though growing in absolute terms). It has led to increasing concern over whether foreign-owned investment in Scottish electronics remains vulnerable to potential investment shifts to lower production cost locations, particularly in Central and Eastern Europe. From a cluster perspective, it has also put a policy priority on deepening the industry's value chain by rooting foreign investors more firmly within the local supply base.

Given the strong agricultural and fishing tradition of the Scottish economy, it is not surprising that the food and drink sector has traditionally been one of the most significant industries in the Scottish economy. With a total workforce of 52,000 people, it accounted for 18 percent of Scottish manufacturing employment and has been one of the leading export sectors in Scotland (Stories and Horne, 1999). However, much of this strength is concentrated in one sub-sector: whisky. Whisky was responsible for over a third of total food and drink turnover, and 85 percent of Scottish exports in the sector.

Despite the core competitive advantage of whisky within the sector, Scottish Enterprise has identified a number of weaknesses in the industry as a whole. In their main market – the UK – Scottish businesses have not been able to supply the higher value added product areas which are increasingly determining the future growth areas of the industry. The industry is characterised by a large pool of small businesses with few large, indigenous companies and low rates of business formation. Apart from whisky, the lack of food processors of suitable scale has meant the sector has remained principally a supplier of raw materials and low value added food products.

Again, in terms of the policy needs of the cluster, it has put emphasis on the need for the industry to shift along its value chain.

Origins of the cluster approach

Traditionally, there has been a strong element of autonomy in Scottish economic development policy, allowing the territory to pursue development strategies distinct from other parts of the UK. Within the British government, a special department – the Scottish Office – existed to oversee a range of government functions in Scotland which were operated by specific departments in England, including health, education and business development. In addition, the Scottish Development Agency (SDA) had been set up to act as a territorial agency with specialised economic development powers. With funding from the Scottish Office, the SDA's activities concentrated on the lowland areas in Scotland, while its sister organisation, the Highlands and Islands Development Board, was responsible for the northern parts of the country.

This two-tiered approach to economic development in Scotland has been subject to periodic revisions. The most recent change has been the recent devolution of power within the UK. The Scottish Parliament was established in 1999 with devolved authority in a wide range of policy areas. In creating a Scottish 'government', the new Parliament has been granted more extensive control over expenditure than hitherto existed in Scotland. As an executive and administrative branch of the new system, the Scottish Office was subsumed within the new Scottish Executive at the same time, again, with the addition of wider policy responsibilities.

However, from the perspective of cluster policy, the key institution has been Scottish Enterprise and its network of local offices. Scottish Enterprise was created in 1991 as a successor to the Scottish Development Agency, with the aim of having a more private sector-influenced approach to economic development (Hayton, 1991). The new network consists of 13 so-called Local Enterprise Companies (LECs) covering different parts of the Scottish lowlands and a centralised headquarters in Glasgow where the main strategy and policy development functions are carried out. A similar system has been put in place for the northern and western parts of Scotland because of the differences in their economic and development challenges: Highlands and Islands Enterprise (HIE). Although many Scottish Enterprise policies have a national scope, for the most part, HIE operates independently within its area.

The cluster approach in Scotland was originally and has consistently been identified with Scottish Enterprise (Danson and Whittam, 1998). Although the approach has evolved over the years, it originated within the agency, was first proselytised by Scottish Enterprise to wider communities and has remained closely linked with its strategic view of its own activities. Indeed, the adoption of the cluster approach in Scottish Enterprise has helped to shape its role in economic development: while this did not entail abandoning the agency's other policy priorities, it has come to be one of the main organising principles for its different policy areas.

First investigated in the early 1990s, the use of cluster analysis in Scottish Enterprise can be largely attributed to the direct and indirect influence of Michael Porter work (for example, Porter, 1990). This was not only evident in the use of the consultancy company in which Porter was involved – Monitor – but the lingering impact of many of his key concepts, notably the 'diamond' model of industry competitiveness and the importance of mapping the value chain links of a cluster. As the cluster concept implies that cluster development is a systemic process, requiring the successful integration of a series of different factors, cluster analysis was important in highlighting the factors which were weak within the system.

The reasons for making use of cluster concepts in economic development derived mainly from the unique economic and policy contexts of Scotland. First, there was a recognition within the agency that the cluster approach could prove a particularly useful tool of economic development. Scottish Enterprise activities have had a common focus on facilitating the emergence of competitive companies within the Scottish economy. Cluster analysis provided a means of analysing the systemic roots of competitiveness for such businesses. Analysis was significant in drawing attention to the existing and potential sources of competitive strength in clusters, particularly in identifying emerging and/or unexploited research strengths in a local economy. It also supported the refinement of policy by assessing where the gaps in the region's clusters lay.

Second, the approach fitted with the agency's existing policy of maximising the value of Scotland's inward investment. While Scotland has been very successful in attracting foreign investment, conversion of these investments into longer-term impacts on indigenous levels of innovation, skills and business activity has proven more difficult. The development of strong, innovation-oriented clusters in Scottish industry would not only help to embed and upgrade the value of existing investment, but would help to attract future, higher-quality projects.

Lastly, the cluster approach supplied what appeared to be a coherent, comprehensive and arguably more effective policy framework for developing Scotland's competitiveness. Scottish Enterprise was increasingly aware of the need to integrate its different policy activities rather than have them exist in isolation from each other. Cluster analysis could support this by enabling policy-makers to understand the different elements contributing to industrial competitiveness.

Interest in cluster development within Scottish Enterprise effectively began with a substantial audit of the Scottish economy. In 1993, Monitor conducted a large-scale study of the economy, applying Porter's cluster concept to the competitiveness of Scotland's industries. Thirty potential clusters were found, from which 13 key sectors were broadly defined, using a variety of indicators including: the world market share of Scottish output; export share within the industry; the size and overall share of employment; overall value added and value added per employee; output growth rates; RTD capability; and the international reputation of the leading firms in Scotland. These statistical measures were combined with more qualitative assessments of the extent to which linkages between businesses occurred in the following areas: product and process design ideas; market intelligence; logistics; and skills training.

The Monitor report provided the basis for future policy developments. The emerging cluster policy focused initially on four pilot sectors, followed by a 'second wave' of targeted clusters drawn from the Monitor cluster list. Different rationales were put forward for choosing the different sectors, but the policy as a whole was bound by several key principles of selection: the economic significance of a cluster; its growth potential; the 'readiness' of the cluster to develop; and the scope for policy to influence cluster development.

There was a time lag between the completion of the Monitor study and the eventual decision to undertake a cluster approach in Scottish Enterprise policy, a period during which the organisation underwent a 'conversion' to the cluster approach. The decision to progress came in 1996 with a paper put before the Scottish Enterprise Board in which an integrated approach to cluster development was promoted with a view to maximising the resources available to the agency (Downes *et al*, 1996). The approach would have several key features. It would be founded on a strong partnership with industry. It was to be based on a value chain understanding of industrial activity rather traditionally-defined sectors and focus on both the links between different clusters and the internal 'engines for growth' within each individual cluster. Moreover, it would not be limited by existing geographically-based responsibilities within the Scottish Enterprise Network.

In 1998, the cluster approach was formally initiated by establishing four 'pilot' cluster teams. Originally, four clusters were selected to 'test' the approach: semiconductors, food and drink, biotechnology, and oil and gas (later reduced to three when it was decided that oil and gas development should be a national rather than a Scottish cluster activity). The four sectors were chosen for different reasons. Semiconductors and oil and gas were perhaps the most obvious choices given the importance of the sectors to the Scottish economy. As well as representing a significant sector in Scotland, the food and drink sector allowed the approach to involve a wide range of participants, particularly in rural areas. Biotechnology represented a good opportunity to apply the approach to a strong potential cluster. Collectively, the four sectors presented a range of cluster types, ranging from emerging (biotechnology) to mature industries (oil and gas), from narrowly defined industries (semiconductors) to broadly-based ones (food and drink). As their industrial structures and cluster needs varied greatly, the likelihood was that the common approach would result in four different sets of policy actions.

In 1999, a second generation of clusters were chosen (Downes and Star, 1999): opto-electronics, forest products, tourism and creative industries. Again, each selection had a different rationale. For opto-electronics, it was recognised that Scotland had key technological strengths in the area and it would complement the semiconductor cluster policy. The forest products sector and tourism have been significant employers across Scotland, but not least in rural areas which may not have much representation in the other cluster areas. Creative and 'knowledge-based' industries contained a number of growing clusters – such as software games – as well as provided strong overlap with other clusters. Other, more limited 'cluster' activities have been undertaken at a local level by individual LECs in chemicals (the Forth Valley), textiles (the Borders) and financial services (Edinburgh).

The seven cluster programmes are to operate in parallel over the same time period: 1999-2004. Approximately €360 million has been allocated to the programmes over that period, representing 11 percent of the Scottish Enterprise operating budget for the same period, if it was assumed that its 2000-01 projected expenditure was held constant over the five-year period. However, it is difficult to estimate cluster budgets fully because of the contributing influence of other non-cluster specific but contributory policy instruments.

To oversee the initial work of the cluster teams, the Cluster Development Directorate was established within Scottish Enterprise. The Directorate had two roles to perform in the emerging cluster policy: to act as a kind of 'missionary' for the cluster approach and become a catalyst for organisational change within the agency; and to provide direct support to the cluster teams in developing their strategies. In addition, the seven programmes will be assessed at the same time within a common evaluation framework.

Despite this activity, when discussing the cluster approach in Scottish Enterprise, it is difficult to refer explicitly to an overall cluster strategy. In many respects, it is more accurate to speak of a series of sector-based strategies, produced by the individual cluster teams, guided by common principles. Cluster policy has largely consisted of the time-limited strategies and action plans produced by the seven individual cluster teams. In spite of their necessary differences though, they have strong similarities in how they have developed the individual policies. First all have undertaken a benchmarking audit of the existing Scottish cluster while researching the main global trends likely to influence the cluster's future development. Second, each cluster strategy involved an extensive process of consultation, especially with the private sector. Each strategy and action plan emerged from a series of workshops held with businesses, where feedback to Scottish Enterprise proposals was critical in refining the policy.

However, the cluster approach has had moderate wider policy impacts. It has informed the policy goals of other parts of Scottish Enterprise. For example, Locate in Scotland – the agency responsible for inward investment promotion – reorganised its activities to focus more specifically on identified priority cluster areas, particularly in the electronics sector (by concentrating on semiconductors and opto-electronics). The influence has not been radical, but it has added a set of horizontal objectives which gives more strategic coherence to the disparate Scottish Enterprise policy activities.

This was initially reflected in the agency's overall strategy. The Network strategy in 1999 contained a clear emphasis on the development of clusters as an agency objective, but one to be maintained alongside other agency priorities (Scottish Enterprise, 1999). However, in the most recent strategy for the organisation, the cluster approach has been clearly limited to the current set of cluster programmes, raising questions about the extent to which it has permanently altered Scottish Enterprise policy (Scottish Enterprise, 2001). Moreover, the Scottish Executive's economic development framework for Scotland as a whole acknowledges the cluster approach, but downplays it against more systemic, Scotland-wide policy priorities (Scottish Executive, 2000b). While the cluster approach has been partially embedded within the Scottish Enterprise network, it has not yet infiltrated Scottish economic development policy as a whole.

The cluster approach in practice

The individual strategies and actions plans of the different cluster teams have applied different approaches as appropriate for each cluster. The number of coordinated measures is large: for example, 90 separate measures are identifiable in the semiconductor action plan. The action plans as a whole display a diverse range of measures, but these can be broadly classified using the typology developed earlier in this volume. The different types of measure address three aspects of cluster development:

- *community-building*, in which cluster identity and identification by its participants is supported;
- *linkages and projects*, where policy assists targeted (often project-specific) networking between sub-groups of firms, research providers and other cluster agents; and
- *common resources*, where the policy creates shared facilities to address a market failure in the cluster.

Examples of the three types can be found in all the cluster strategies, but by way of illustration, Table 8.1 below focuses on the three pilot clusters.

Many of these measures have existed – or would have been carried forward – without the cluster approach. For example, the Alba Centre, one of the flagship projects of the semiconductor cluster, predates the approach. The Centre is a specially-designed research/design institute and science park which was developed jointly by Scottish Enterprise and the foreign investor, Cadence Design Systems. Its development was regarded as central to addressing the product design weaknesses in the Scottish industry and ensuring the continuing strength of the semiconductors sector. The cluster approach, however, has been able to build on this project by providing a framework for attaching and designing other policies which would enhance its effectiveness, such as creating the Institute for System Level Integration within the Centre, a joint university organisation set up to provide training in chip design, and expanding the infrastructure premises available for chip-based companies.

Table 8.1: Examples of different types of measures in cluster programmes in Scotland

Semiconductors	
Community-building	*Semiconductor Supplier Forum*: developing new association for the industry through business-based working groups and workshops
Linkages/projects	Assessing the scope for sharing the costs for a new semiconductor manufacturing facility among a partnership of firms
Common resources	*Alba Centre*: continued property/services infrastructure support for the semiconductor design facility at the Alba Centre
	Institute for System Level Integration: a joint Scottish universities collaboration to provide specific engineering degree programmes in Systems Level Integration (part of the Alba Centre)
Food and drink	
Community-building	Enhance the biotechnology 'organics' sub-cluster by considering how to market Scotland's image in the sector more effectively
Linkages/projects	Support for cooperation initiatives in collective branding and market entry
Common resources	*Scottish Food and Drink Consumer and Market Intelligence Centre*: set up to providing intelligence to the whole cluster
	Virtual Food and Drink College: investigate potential for linking existing learning organisation training courses together
Biotechnology	
Community-building	*Scottish BioAlliance*: create an industry organisation for the cluster
Linkages/projects	Encourage networking of specialist support providers, such as financial and legal advisors
Common resources	*INNOVOL*: a database of all Scottish life science researchers
	Development of an independent applied research centre

The example is illustrative of the cluster approach's impact throughout the cluster strategies. In some cases, the strategies have identified the scope for extending existing successful measures and projects. In other cases, different sets of measures have been linked together to improve their effectiveness (such as engineering training with the development of the Alba Centre above). Cluster analysis also revealed the scope for developing new initiatives to address the problems that surfaced in the economic audit and consultation phases of the strategies. Some clusters contained a larger number of new measures than others – particularly where the industries were receiving targeted public support for the first time (such as biotechnology and creative industries) – but the importance of the cluster approach has not been the extent to which it induced new policy measures, but its role in providing a framework for integrating all policy activity in support of cluster development. Policy coordination rather than creation has been the most important benefit of the cluster approach in Scotland.

Despite the diversity, several points can be highlighted about the common approaches to implementing policy evident under the different programmes. The programmes have often relied on existing policies and projects, brought together under the umbrella of the cluster action plans, but in providing policy 'value added', the strategies have been careful to minimise the timespan and scale of policy interventions. Implementation has also been overseen by special plan delivery groups, composed of both public and private sector members, but overall, the strategies have stressed the voluntary nature of private sector involvement in the actions.

As public-private partnerships, the strategies have outlined key responsibilities for Scottish Enterprise, the private sector and other institutions. Across each of the cluster programmes, these different roles can be discussed as a whole.

Once the strategies have been put in place, it is envisaged that policy delivery will shift away from the main office of Scottish Enterprise (Scottish Enterprise National). While many cluster activities continue to be pursued at the centre – particularly through the centralised functions of export and FDI promotion carried out by the units within Scottish Enterprise network – for the most part, the centre's role in cluster policy has been viewed as largely been a coordinating and catalytic one. Indeed, for several cluster programmes, the group overseeing the strategy's progress has been rolled out of Scottish Enterprise. Greater responsibility for implementing the action plans lies with the individual LECs within the Scottish Enterprise network.

For the LECs as a whole, the adoption of the cluster approach has been voluntarist and to some extent, piecemeal. It contrasts with their traditional activities of simply delivering standardised core Scottish Enterprise policies within their locality. Indeed, the new approach has been instrumental in creating new opportunities for dialogue with the companies and organisations within the LEC area, raising their credibility – both as participants of a larger network strategy and in terms of the greater industry knowledge the cluster approach fosters – and encouraging more business input into policy design. Where individual LECs have taken part in the cluster programmes, it has largely depended on the importance of the cluster within the local area. However, their involvement has not been at a strictly geographical level: LECs with a particular concentration of the cluster industry or a recognised expertise have been given responsibility for parts of the different programmes, as cluster team leaders are chosen from across the network rather than within Scottish Enterprise National. It is part of a wider effort to integrate the Scottish Enterprise network, shifting from a strictly geographical to a more functional approach to economic development.

Central to the different cluster strategies has been the private sector's involvement. In developing the strategy, it was critical that the cluster's participants felt that they had ownership of the strategy, allowing the public sector's role in cluster development to be limited to the initial impetus not ongoing intervention. Extensive consultation characterised the different cluster programmes, though levels of enthusiasm differed depending on the sector. For example, the willingness of businesses in the forest industry to become involved in the development and implementation of their cluster strategy appears to have been more marked than in the semiconductor sector, where some of the key industrial players have been less likely to see themselves as part of a wider cluster. Similarly, where the cluster is diffuse and extensive, it can be difficult to develop a common cluster identity – a problem, for example, in the tourism cluster.

In large part, the differences have reflected the capacity of the programme to develop an industry community around the strategy. Where this has been easier to achieve, several factors have supported a widespread acceptance of policy action. It has been important that the industry recognises either their common vulnerability to external competition or the opportunity for collective action bringing industry-wide benefits. Support for the strategy has also been more forthcoming either where the industry is used to acting collectively – especially through existing industry associations, such as the Scottish Electronics Forum (in the case of semiconductors) – or where the industries are sufficiently new and based on common research resources that the main players tend to know each other, as is the case in biotechnology.

In many cases, even where the industry has been an active partner in developing a cluster programme, it has not necessarily been with the same objective as the public sector. Common to all the cluster strategies has been the problem of conveying the cluster concept to the private sector. Businesses have been receptive to some of its constituent ideas – for example, the importance of networking – but it is not clear that the private sector shares the same vision of becoming self-sustaining, highly competitive clusters. The value of the approach has often been perceived in terms of one-off externalities arising from individual projects and a systematic response to new market and technology trends. Indeed, there has been a tendency for Scottish Enterprise not to employ 'cluster' language in developing several of the strategies. Within the action plans, responsibility for certain measures has already been earmarked for the private sector. However, at least in the initial stages of policy implementation, the role of companies is anticipated to be mainly participatory.

Conclusions

Cluster policy in Scotland has only now been brought to the point of implementation, so it is too early to appraise its operation (Scottish Enterprise itself is currently planning its own mid-term evaluation of its progress). Comments can be made about its design though. The policy has had a long gestation period – seven years separate the Monitor report on the Scottish economy's cluster potential and the acceptance of the last action plans for the seven clusters in 2000. Indeed, the Scottish approach to developing the policy has been marked by careful preparation and a well-planned, step-by-step progression through the designing of the strategies, their delivery mechanisms and arrangements for their evaluation. In light of the substantial attention which has been given to the policy's foundations, there is scope for believing that the seven action plans are likely to have realistic and eminently achievable goals in their outputs. Whether the policy as a whole will have longer-term impacts in the clusters themselves remains to be seen.

Scottish cluster policy has been clearly-defined, detailed and costed. Considerable efforts have gone into building consensus around its priorities and securing commitment to its actions with relevant actors in both the public and private sectors. While set up as a new and largely autonomous policy area, care has been taken to ensure its priorities influence and take account of the goals of related policy areas. Not surprisingly then, of the case-study policies in this volume, Scotland's has not only been one of the most well-publicised and projected of cluster policies, it also been one of the most systematic. This success in policy design can be seen at each level of the policy: its overall strategic structure; its constituent cluster programmes; and the individual measures which are supported.

The *strategic framework* of the policy has been designed to realise the possibilities of the cluster approach while recognising the realities of the existing policy structure in Scotland. The value of the framework can be seen at every stage of policy-making in Scotland. Detailed economic analysis underlies the policy: the economy as a whole has been examined for its cluster potential and the individual clusters themselves have been subject to detailed expert studies and benchmarking. Cluster selection took account of the economy's existing and future strengths as well as the scope for policy to affect their development. The subsequent policy has been structured with a series of complementary elements, organising the existing policy areas of the Scottish Enterprise Network around a set of cluster foci. It has relatively clear timetables for actions, with the different cluster programmes operating in parallel but to the same timescales. Policy responsibilities and budgets at measure and programme level are clearly articulated. The policy has even learnt lessons from its own experience. It has undergone a pilot testing period with the original four cluster areas: while this was not sufficient for testing the economic impacts of the approach, the experience in developing the four pilot strategies has fed into strategy-making for the second wave of cluster programmes.

At the level of the *individual cluster strategies or programmes*, the policy has also shown clear strategic principles. Consultation in the strategy has been strongly emphasised during policy development, recognising its importance as the first step to gathering the necessary commitment from the various private, public and research actors essential for its implementation. The strategies have also been designed with a view to minimising the scale and length of public intervention with clear timetables and benchmarking measures. The principles of self-help have been projected from the start: in forcing the private sector to take greater responsibility for setting the strategies' agendas and participating in their projects and measures, the strategies have already begun the slow process of cluster identity-building.

At the level of *measures and projects*, again, the cluster strategies have combined a diverse set of measures around their main priorities. These priorities have been used to organise both 'old' projects as well as suggesting the areas where new ones need to be developed. In scope, they deal with the major aspects of cluster development: community-building; support for specific linkages; and the development of common resources for the cluster. Particular efforts have also been made to identify the key measures in each priority or strategy and to build other measures around them in order to maximise their impact (as can be seen in the example of the Alba Centre in the semiconductors strategy).

Lastly, the strategic approach has negotiated the notoriously difficult area of monitoring and evaluating cluster policy. While there are difficult methodological challenges remaining to be solved, the Scottish approach has at least in place an evaluation structure which should provide adequate tracking of the policy's progress, a reflection of the *efficiency* of policy and the first steps towards measuring its *effectiveness* in the economy as a whole.

The successful features of the cluster policy – its coherence, structure and apparent relevance – can be attributed to a series of factors relating to the conduct and structure of policy-making in Scotland. First, the policy has had a powerful champion in Scottish Enterprise. Within the UK – and to a large extent, internationally – Scottish Enterprise is one of the most powerful regional development agencies. The agency has been able to commit significant resources to the policy, bringing to the approach the benefit of its wide portfolio of economic development powers. It also has an extensive geographical network, which has provided a relatively effective system for policy delivery as well as a source of intelligence on the local development of parts of its target clusters. Within the agency as a whole, there is a substantial amount of industry and policy expertise.

Second, the policy has been successfully promoted by the traditions of networking and partnership in Scotland. Within Scotland, there is a long history of partnership between public and private sectors (in the latter case, both employers and trade unions) in the area of economic development. When Scottish Enterprise was established, its remit included a strong degree of private sector partnership, and in the eyes of many in the policy-making community, the 'corporate' image of Scottish Enterprise continues to reflect its internal culture. Moreover, despite the tensions over cluster policy with other major public sector bodies, the absence of consensus on the approach has not hindered the everyday practical experience of cooperation on individual projects. While some policy-makers may disagree with Scottish Enterprise on its rationale for the cluster strategies, the value of the measures themselves has largely not been disputed.

Policy and institutional factors, then, have supported cluster development policy in Scotland. It is less obvious whether the territory's *economic* factors have supported it as well. Indeed, as a whole, while Scotland demonstrates relatively high levels of efficiency in cluster policy-making, the overall effectiveness of policy has yet to be tested. While acknowledging the strength of cluster analysis in providing clear indications of the opportunities and problems facing the different Scottish clusters, there are three sets of general weaknesses of the Scottish economy which will shape the cluster policy's ability to achieve its ends: the Scottish research base; its lack of a networking tradition; and the more systemic problems in the Scottish economy.

Cluster development depends on a range of factors, but two of the most important are the presence of research advantages and the ability of firms to link their own competitiveness to them. The Scottish research base is strong in many of the cluster areas, as demonstrated by its high profile in many of the cluster strategies. However, as a whole, it is characterised by a relative lack of linkages with industry. Scotland (in common with the UK as a whole) has not developed strong traditions of industry-academic cooperation (Scottish Executive, 2000c). As a result, in general, there has been less commercialisation of the research base than is satisfactory, there has not been enough applied industrial research and the ability of universities to respond directly to the training needs of companies has been limited. The cluster strategies have directly tackled these issues, building on a range of recent public and research sector initiatives which have already started to change this environment.

Networking is not only low between research providers and the industrial community, but among firms themselves, cooperation is not widespread. The habit of 'clustering' which should be at the core of cluster development has only been pronounced in isolated individual initiatives within industries (as in the oil and gas industry, which has long acted collectively) or in new, emerging sectors which are driven by their research and innovation requirements (as, for example, opto-electronics, which developed its own industry association before cluster policy). Within Scotland as a whole, the culture of interfirm cooperation has been slow to develop, a manifestation perhaps of an industrial tradition dominated by large-firm employers.

Finally, the Scottish economy continues to suffer from a series of more systemic problems. Relatively low productivity performance and levels of entrepreneurship have been continuing sources of concern to policy-makers.[21] Much of the economy remains tied to foreign-owned investment and ownership, making it vulnerable to a range of external factors beyond the influence of policy. The extent to which the Scottish cluster policy will help to solve – rather than be hindered – by some (if not all) of these problems will be one of the principal tests of the approach.

Note

[21] Such problems have been given clear prominence in the Scottish Executive's recent economic strategy for the whole of Scotland, *The Way Forward* (Scottish Executive, 2000b).

Chapter 9

Styria

Christian Hartmann

Introduction

In the national and international media the regional economy of Styria is nowadays associated with the successful and dynamic development of its automobile cluster. It has a reputation as a successful location for international investment in the automobile industry: as well as well-known suppliers such as Magna Auteca, the Georg Fischer Mössner group, Johnson Controls and the Lear Corporation, several large car producers (such as Daimler Chrysler, GM and BMW) have also located in the area. However, this success has been a recent phenomenon. However, in the 1980s, the prevailing image of Styria was that of Upper Styria: a mature, declining industrial area characterised by poor future prospects and u·iemployment rates much higher than the national average (as shown in Fig·ire 9.1).

Figure 9.1: Unemployment rate in Styria in percent (1986–98)

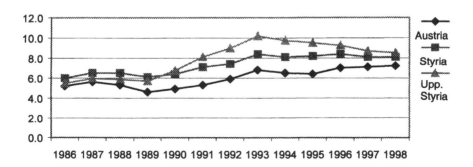

Between these two almost contrasting pictures arguably lies the successful introduction of clusters as a new policy instrument in the 1990s.

Amongst other factors, the application of the cluster approach helped to give new perspectives to Styrian economic and political leaders, contributing to the emergence of a new philosophy for regional economic development. As a result, the cluster approach has influenced the economic promotion strategies of Styrian policy-makers, with policy activities now focused on the development of collaboration between firms and RTD institutions (especially in the automobile industry). The use of the cluster approach is not limited to automobiles though, but extends to other branches of the regional economy such as IT and wood products.

Despite the apparent upturn in the region's fortunes and successful development of the automobile cluster, the approach as a whole is still being tested. The following chapter outlines progress in the use of the cluster approach in Styria, providing an overview of its origins as well as factors behind its differential performance in different Styrian clusters.

The economic context of the cluster approach

General background

Through the 1980s and early 1990s, Styria suffered from low levels of growth in its regional output. This gap in the growth rate had been mainly caused by two factors: the crisis of the steel industry in Upper Styria; and the generally unfavourable geographical position of Styria in the periphery of Western Europe.

The problems of the steel industry in Upper Styria turned out to be the major bottleneck for economic development in Styria in the period preceding the focus on cluster development. The region was dominated by large state-owned firms that were highly vertically integrated and had lost their headquarter functions to Vienna in the 1960s and 1970s, resulting in Styrian plants increasingly coming under 'external' control. In most cases, planning, RTD and marketing/distribution functions – i.e. those responsible for the monitoring of markets and technology – were relocated out of the region (Tödtling and Sedlarcek, 1997). As a result, many firms lost their autonomous capacity to innovate and adapt to changes in their macro-environment. At the same time, the resulting decline in large firms undergoing restructuring was not compensated by new firm formation. The Styrian economy faced severe structural problems as regional output decreased dramatically and the rate of unemployment rose (Figure 9.2). Up to the early 1990s, it seemed that no sector of the Styrian economy could compensate for these losses of output and employment.

Figure 9.2: Changes in regional output in Styria (1986-95)

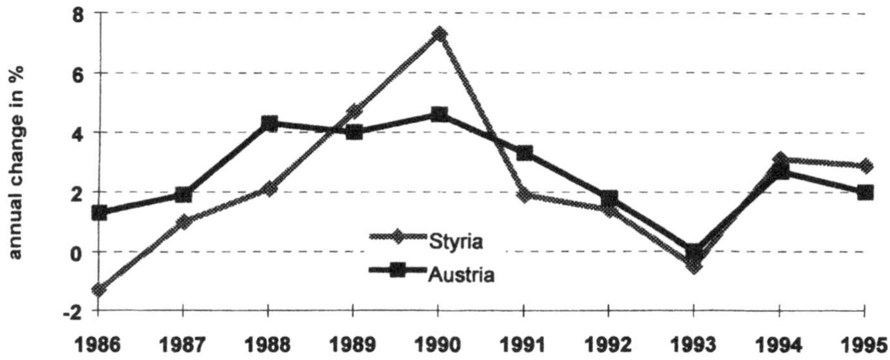

In the 1990s several changes reshaped the economic environment of the Styrian economy. With the opening of countries in Central and Eastern European (CEE) and the integration of Austria into the EU, the position of Styria suddenly shifted from the rim to the centre of Europe. Styria became a bridgehead into CEE and began to attract more foreign direct investment aiming to develop those markets.

However, these changes also brought challenges to Styrian firms. The globalisation of economic activity and an increasing international division of labour made necessary the formation and implementation of new strategies. Firms needed to learn to collaborate and develop the potential to innovate as a strategic resource. Yet the region's success in coping with these challenges is evident, as can be seen in its growth of regional output which exceeded the Austrian average in 1994 (and indeed, all other Austrian regions) (Figure 9.2). Much of this change can be attributed to growth in several key, cluster-based industries in the region.

Styrian cluster industries[22]

Currently five branches of the Styrian economy can been seen as cluster industries. These clusters either have strong regional input linkages (i.e. significantly higher than the average of the Styrian economy) or are characterised by relatively high growth rates in output and employment (i.e. growth above Austrian and Styrian averages). Altogether the clusters have significantly higher shares of knowledge-intensive collaborative links with other firms and the regional RTD infrastructure than the average for Styrian industry as a whole (Figure 9.3).

The five Styrian clusters are: the automobile industry, especially motor vehicle manufacture (NACE 341); the chemical/pharmacological industry, especially basic chemicals (NACE 241); the metal machine-building industry with a special focus on basic iron and steel and ferro-alloys (NACE 271); the wood/paper industry, especially sawmilling and planing, impregnation of wood, and carpentry and joinery (NACE 201, 203); and IT with a special focus on software (NACE 722) (Adametz *et al*, 1998).

Growth in employment and real output has been particularly strong for the automobile cluster. From 1995 to 1998, the number of employees grew by 23 percent (as opposed to a national average of 6 percent) while real output grew by 92 percent (against a national average of 26 percent). In 1998, the core of this cluster comprised about 60 firms with 7,900 employees, producing an annual output of ATS 35 billion (€2.5 billion). Nevertheless, relative to other clusters, the automobile cluster is characterised by rather weak regional embeddedness: in 1998, only 17 percent of the input to its firms was provided by regionally-based enterprises, while the cluster exported 95 percent of its output. On the other hand, this cluster has a strong orientation towards the highly-developed regional knowledge infrastructure: more than 58 percent of its firms in 1998 claimed to collaborate regularly with universities and other regional RTD institutions (above the Styrian average of 13 percent).

In recent years, the chemicals/pharmaceuticals cluster has also shown growth in real output of 37 percent (contrasting with Austria as a whole, 10 percent). Employment has risen at a rate of 10 percent (as compared to a *decline* in Austria of 3 percent). In 1998, this cluster consisted of 50 firms with 1,670 employees, producing an annual output of ATS 4.2 billion (€305 million). More than 73 percent of the firms have claimed to collaborate regularly with the regional knowledge infrastructure (again, compared to the average for all Styrian industry, 13 percent). With regards to the regional embeddedness of this cluster, again its firms receive only 17 percent of their inputs from regional suppliers.

Figure 9.3: Regional input linkages and knowledge-intensive collaboration in Styrian clusters

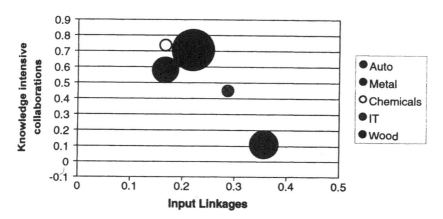

In contrast, employment in the metal/machine-building-cluster has fallen by two percent in recent years, slightly faster than the national average (a fall of one percent). The growth of real output of the metal cluster (15 percent) has been also below the national average (20 percent). This cluster was made up of 450 firms with 20,500 employees, generating ATS 44.8 billion (€3.3 billion)in output. However, despite limited recent growth, the cluster exhibits stronger regional embeddedness – its firms source 22 percent of their inputs from regional suppliers and more than 70 percent of firms collaborate regularly with universities and other RTD institutions.

The wood/paper cluster has also shrunk in employment recently, with a fall of four percent (more than the national average of only one percent). However, the growth of real output (11 percent) has been larger than the national average (8 percent). The core of the cluster comprises 560 firms with 9,400 employees, producing an output of ATS 12.8 billion (€0.9 billion). The cluster has strong regional embeddedness, with 36 percent of its firms' input coming from Styrian suppliers. At the same time, it has a poor performance in terms of knowledge intensive collaborations: only 11 percent of companies have collaborated with higher educational organisations and RTD institutions on a regular basis (less than the Styrian average of 13 percent).

Lastly, in terms of employment, the IT cluster has grown rapidly (44 percent), though not as much as the national average (51 percent). It consists of about 500 firms with 1,600 employees and an output of ATS 1.5

billion (€109 million). Again, the cluster displays a strong regional embeddedness with 29 percent of inputs coming from Styrian enterprises. At the same time, the cluster is also closely tied to the regional knowledge infrastructure: 45 percent of enterprises have collaborated with regional suppliers of knowledge on a regular basis.

Origins of the cluster approach

The new philosophy for regional economic policies in the 1990s

At the beginning of the 1990s, a new philosophy for economic policy was developing in Styria, growing out of the experience of the crisis in the Upper Styrian steel industry. During the 1980s, economic development had principally meant support to large firms under pressure and the attraction of foreign direct investment, policy instruments which were largely associated with financial subsidies from the government. Policy had largely consisted of the reactive allocation of public funds. However, the new philosophy brought three new perspectives into the discussion.

The first perspective was a decline in the simple promotion of business investments. In future, a new 'softer' approach to development activities was to substitute the 'old-style' policy. 'Soft' promotion meant the support of immaterial, intangible goods instead of 'harder' physical capital investments. Thus regional economic policy and its instruments were refocused on the pro-active support of collaboration, the stimulation of innovative behaviour, the transfer of technology and knowledge, and the provision of consulting services to firms. Moreover, future programmes would thus address networks and intermediaries instead of single firms.

The second perspective addressed the issue of endogenous economic potential. If the past was devoted to the attraction of FDI, now it was the regional potential of firms and elements of the regional innovation infrastructure which became the goals of policy. Out of this new orientation arose a demand for information concerning the regional strengths of the Styrian economy.

The third perspective dealt with the conception of economic policy itself. In the past, policy setting had been a top-down process performed solely by public administration. Other economic actors were restricted to the role of applicants for support. Within the new philosophy though, it was conceived that policy delivery would take place through 'one stop shops' offering services to firms. Policy implementation should be performed in lean flexible organisations instead of 'sluggish' governmental bodies. Thus a need for new organisational structures for regional policy arose. Consequently, in 1991, the Styrian industrial promotion agency (SFG) was founded with the aim of providing an efficient and independent office for industrial promotional activities. It was intended to complement the Department of Economic Policy within the regional government as a lean flexible agency acting as a service provider to Styrian enterprises. The SFG was organised as a limited company with the government of the province of Styria as its only shareholder. Its tasks comprised the management of industrial promotion activities and the implementation of regional technology policy measures. Since 1996, it has been in charge of all operational activities related to economic policy and thus has been also responsible for the implementation of Styrian cluster development efforts.

These new perspectives together paved the way for a new understanding of regional policy. They led to substantial changes in the organisational framework for regional policy in Styria, allowing for the provision of new policy instruments. They also created the groundwork for the development of the cluster approach within Styrian economic development policy.

The cluster approach in the concept of regional policy in Styria

In the 1990s, two related strategies provided key ideas which shaped the understanding of clusters held by regional policy actors in Styria. These two sets of ideas can be classified as Porterian. Clusters were understood in both strategies as consisting of a large number of enterprises that are interconnected through input and collaborative technological links. At the centre of such clusters are highly competitive producers of final goods, complemented by a ring of supporting and related industries which altogether form an extensive value chain for final goods (Porter, 1990a). This image of clusters also implied specific policy recommendations that were brought forth in the two strategies – or 'policy concepts' – as discussed in detail below.

The cluster approach in the Styrian Technology Policy Concept. In 1993, the Institute of Technology and Regional Policy, part of Joanneum Research, was commissioned by the regional ministries for economic policy and science and technology to prepare a regional technology strategy. Completed in 1995, this strategy was a response to similar developments in other European regions (such as Bavaria). As well as providing general technology policy recommendations, it also contained a detailed catalogue of innovation related measures as technology policy was seen as a way to cope with the challenges of the Styrian economy.

The Styrian Technology Policy Concept can be characterised as highly cluster-orientated in all its recommendations and measures. Clusters were seen in this concept as the principal focus of policy impacts, and thus the concept recommended a focus on clusters instead of single enterprises (Steiner *et al*, 1996). A major advantage of such a cluster oriented approach was that the high leverage of policy measures was emphasised: impacts could spread rapidly through the inter-firm linkages present in a cluster. Another advantage was seen in the ability of regional clusters to link into international networks and thus participate in the exchange of new knowledge/technologies. The cluster orientation implied two basic categories of policy measures for Styrian enterprises: measures to strengthen further the competitiveness of already existing clusters; and measures to foster the formation of new clusters in promising industrial sectors.

Because of this strong emphasis on clusters in Styrian technology policy, significant analytical effort was put into the identification of clusters in the regional economy. In addition to analysing secondary statistical data, a survey of Styrian enterprises was carried out, focusing on their innovative and collaborative behaviour. Through this approach, five clusters were identified and specific policy recommendations prepared, as summarised below (Steiner *et al*, 1996).

- For *the raw materials cluster*, existing collaborative activities between leading firms and regional RTD institutions should be further intensified to enhance innovation and new technology based firms should be integrated into already existing networks.
- For *the wood/paper cluster*, collaboration should be fostered mainly in the field of marketing and linkages to national and international networks should be developed.
- Within *the transportation cluster*, a special focus should be made on the automobile sector. Intensifying collaborative links could bring significant opportunities for the cluster in future while the development of system solutions (e.g. with respect to the manufacture of engines or powertrains) could greatly improve its existing strong competitiveness.
- For *the environmental technology cluster* (encompassing environmental engineering, wastewater treatment, woodchip furnaces etc.), collaborative links should be intensified and international networks fostered in order to improve the competitiveness of this cluster.
- Lastly, for *the alternative energy cluster*, joint projects with the transportation and environmental technology clusters should be promoted in order to develop synergies between these sectors.

To encourage collaboration, pilot umbrella projects for each cluster were recommended. Within these umbrella projects two instruments were applied: the use of IT and networking workshops in the clusters; and the financial support of ongoing collaborative projects. As a result, the Technology Policy Concept and its recommendations were influential for the conduct of the cluster development projects that followed. In particular the strong emphasis on a new pro-active 'soft' approach to economic promotion and policy implementation was significant.

The 'cluster portfolio' approach of IWI. In addition to the Technology Policy Concept, strategic policy guidelines addressing all sectors of the Styrian economy were also prepared by the IWI (Institute for Industrial Policy). In 1994, it developed a study of the Styrian economy on behalf of the Department of Economic Policy and the Styrian chamber of commerce. The objective was to identify the distinct strengths and potential of the regional economy in order to focus future policy efforts. To fulfil this task, the IWI adopted a new methodology developed for regional policy-makers and used the cluster approach to identify the regional economy's potential strengths.

The IWI had already pioneered cluster analysis for Austria as a whole, deriving their approach from the work of Porter (Bellak and Weiss, 1992). Clusters should be highly competitive and strongly export oriented, while at the same time, 'visible' from an analytical perspective (Weiss, 1994). Identifying clusters involved highlighting those parts of the economy with above-average shares of exports (as an indicator of competitiveness) and correspondingly above-average shares of employees in the regional economic structure (as an indicator of regional clustering). For the analysis of Styria, this national approach had to regionalised (Fabris *et al*, 1996). The analysis was completed in 1995 with a total of seven identified clusters that were deemed worthy of further investigation (as strong or semi-strong clusters): transportation; wood/paper; raw materials; IT; textiles; medical technology; construction; and electrical power supply.

The new approach also introduced a new understanding of how regional policy could be formed. Policy makers should, in a way analogous to the strategic managers of large corporations, view economic policy in terms of a portfolio. Policy support – and thus public funds – should only be concentrated on those portfolio elements (i.e. clusters) which promise the most significant future return in development terms. This feature of the IWI approach was particularly appealing to the Styrian government and resulted in implementation of a cluster approach for the Styrian economy.

The cluster approach in practice

On the basis of this new philosophy for regional policy, two clusters have been developed in Styria to date: the automobile cluster (or AC Styria); and the wood cluster. Both developments reflect the implications of this new approach but illustrate at the same time its limitations.

The Styrian Automobile Cluster (AC Styria)

The origin of the AC Styria dates back to 1994 when the survey of Styrian clusters conducted by IWI identified a transportation cluster with a high potential for growth, comprising both the automobile and the public transport industry. Based on this study, the government of Styria decided to focus its cluster oriented policy activities on the automobile industry which seemed to be more promising in its performance outlook than the other identified clusters. The subsequent development of the AC Styria comprises three consecutive stages spanning the period 1995-2000.

1st stage of development – formation of a detailed cluster strategy. In late 1995, Trigon – a team of Austrian consultants – was appointed to identify concrete starting points for the development of a cluster in the Styrian automobile industry. The project had several goals and outputs. First, a company database was established in order to get an overview of potential future cooperation partners for the cluster's development. Second, relevant trends for the automobile sector were analysed as an information base for a direct approach to firms. Third, common issues and problems in the automobile sector were identified as a basis for future collaborative links and projects. Finally, strategy recommendations for the development of an Styrian automobile cluster had to be provided to the SFG.

In order to fulfil these objectives the following steps were taken. Initially, a total of 100 firms and regional RTD institutions were surveyed. This survey was based on the current trends and developments in the automobile sector both at national and international level. In a second step, a SWOT analysis was performed as a basis for future strategies and measures involving a catalogue of measures, prepared by the project team and presented to the interviewed firms for comment and feedback. In the third step, a working group consisting of experts and firm representatives integrated the feedback and honed the final version of the catalogue. The study in its final version recommended four key actions for the development of a Styrian automobile cluster (Trigon, 1996):

- better information and communication;
- initiation of projects to support collaboration;
- setting up an inter-company learning 'club'; and
- special cluster related public relations.

2nd stage – cluster development through an external consultant. In late 1996, a cluster development project for the automobile industry in Styria, based on the study by Trigon, was launched. It was agreed that this development phase should have a duration of two years (i.e. until 1998). In 1998, this development phase was then prolonged until 2000 to ensure the cluster was self-supporting. A total budget of ATS 11.5 million (€0.8 million) – was provided to the Styrian industrial promotion agency (SFG) by the Styrian government for this pilot project. The SFG appointed AGIPLAN – a German-based consulting firm with experience in cluster management and inter-firm collaboration – as operational manager of the project.

In order to have a lean organisation that could still cope with the complexity of a cluster development, a threefold structure was chosen. Overall responsibility for the project lay with SFG. AGIPLAN was to develop the individual cluster activities in close co-ordination and communication with the SFG. The third and most important body for the cluster development process was the advisory committee. This committee was composed of high-ranking delegates from leading companies, SMEs, politicians, researchers and representatives of other institutions. This advisory committee fixed the focus of work and ensured concrete results in the planned cluster projects. As a result, four fields for strategic action were defined for the further development of the cluster:

- improvement of information and communication for the cluster members ('Communication and Information');
- initiation of collaboration between firms and/or regional RTD institutions ('Collaboration');
- qualification/development of the knowledge base ('Qualification'); and
- marketing of the cluster and the location of Styria ('Marketing').

In all four fields, projects were designed and implemented together with cluster firms, regional RTD institutions and international partners.

In the field 'Communication and Information', about 35 theme-specific workshops per year were organised by AGIPLAN. The themes ranged from the implementation of 'Gemba Kaizen' (continuous quality improvement) to particular engineering techniques (e.g. squeeze casting with new materials such as magnesium). Besides the informational dimension, the major aim of these workshops was the development of a culture of collaboration between the firms as a prerequisite for the second set of cluster actions.

In the field 'Collaboration', an internet-based database for collaboration was set up. This database matched potential partner firms in the cluster and provided information about ongoing projects to the other members of AC Styria. About 50 collaborative projects were carried out within the cluster, covering a wide range of areas: from the development of new car components to developing a clearing-house between different standards for EDI (electronic data interchange).

In the field 'Qualification', several inter-firm projects were developed and implemented. The themes of these projects comprised, for example, the implementation of a training network for CATIA (a CAD software package), internet-based courses in English for engineers and training in total quality management.

Lastly, in the field 'Marketing', roadshows presenting the AC Styria were organised in several European capital cities (as well in key US cities such as Detroit). These activities also aimed at attracting new investors in the automobile industry to Styria.

3rd stage – shift to a self-supporting organisational structure. In 2000, the organisational structure of the cluster management was changed in order to realise the planned self supporting status of the cluster. Thus the appointment to AGIPLAN was not renewed and the legal status of AC Styria was changed to that of a limited company. The shareholders of this new limited company were: the SFG; four leading firms of the Styrian Automobile Industry (Magna International, AVL, TCM and Krenhof); AGIPLAN; and the Styrian Association of Industrial Enterprises. Again, the newly formed advisory committee has to define the scope of work, integrate the interests and activities of different groups within the cluster and act as a feedback loop for the different cluster projects. The operational development and management tasks of AC Styria are now performed by the general manager of AC Styria Ltd. The strategic key actions of this self-supporting cluster are, according to its mission statement, to:

- strengthen the cooperation between public facilities, politics and the economy within the net product chain – Public Private Partnership;
- provide the partners of AC Styria with first class communication and an information platform;
- promote the image of AC Styria and by so doing, improve the image of Styria as a location for the automobile industry;

- expand current networks, making them available to more cluster participants;
- form interest groups and initiate cooperation projects in order to achieve cost saving synergy effects;
- make technology and information transfer possible;
- initiate vocational and educational programs with a view towards the future; and
- promote the middle-term strategic orientation of an automotive cluster in Styria.

The self-supporting status of the cluster also has implications for the participating firms. While the membership in the development phase did not place any financial obligations on firms, this has since changed. Firms and institutions that want to benefit from full membership (called 'the impulse package') of the cluster now have to pay an annual fee of at least ATS 7,000 (approximately €500) – up to a maximum of ATS 100,000 (approximately €7,100), the actual sum depending on the annual turnover of the firm. This membership status offers access to restricted information networks, an inter-company learning platform, a total quality management club and other club goods offered by the cluster management. As of 2001, AC Styria has about 153 paying members with plans to increase this number further. In addition to these 153 member firms the cluster comprises another 250 firms that act as (non-paying) partners. They participate in joint projects and networks but are restricted in their access to the services offered to the full members.

The wood cluster in Styria

The origin of the Styrian wood cluster also dates back to 1994 when the survey of Styrian Clusters conducted by IWI identified a 'wood and paper' cluster with a moderate potential for growth, comprising the wood-processing and the paper production industry. The government of Styria decided to focus its policy activities on the wood processing sector, as this already had a strong business association that could be used as a platform for the cluster's management. Encouraged by visible success of AC Styria, the authorities decided in 1997 to start another cluster development process. However, this process lacked the rapidity of development of the automobile cluster, as the stages of development between 1997 and 2001 were marked by a series of difficulties in establishing a wood cluster.

1st stage of development – formation of a detailed cluster strategy. In 1997, Trigon was commissioned to develop a new cluster strategy by identifying concrete starting points for the development of a cluster in the wood processing sector. The design of this project was different from the analogous phase in the development of the automobile cluster. In the case of the wood cluster, Trigon collaborated closely with PRO HOLZ Styria, the regional branch of a business association of Austrian wood processing firms and farmers. PRO HOLZ Styria was already working on issues such as collaboration between firms and RTD institutions. Thus, Trigon based their study on existing approaches developed by PRO HOLZ Styria.

Nevertheless, severe problems arose during the project: the wood processing sector turned out to be considerably more heterogeneous than the automobile industry as the cluster was highly fragmented in different regional and thematic subgroups. As a consequence, the team experienced significant difficulties in finding issues and problems shared by all the firms. In addition, a culture of collaboration and trust was poorly developed – most leading firms in this cluster tended to act in isolation.

A total of 30 interviews with firms and other key actors in the cluster were conducted. Finally, two sub-clusters with the likelihood of sufficient potential for further development were identified, defined as 'innovative approaches to construction with wood' and 'wood-based renewable energy systems'. Again, a working group was set up to identify strategies and measures for the two sub-clusters and they proposed four strategic key actions for the two clusters (Trigon, 1997):

- development of a common and accessible information base for all actors in the cluster, containing information about technologies and markets;
- initiating collaborative projects between firms and/or RTD institutions;
- initiating intra- and inter-company learning with new tools and methods; and
- marketing and public relations for the cluster.

2nd stage – scrutinising the willingness to collaborate in the sub-cluster 'innovative approaches to construction with wood'. In late 1997, it was decided to start another preparatory project for the development of the wood cluster. The objective of this project was to scrutinise the potential of inter-firm collaboration in the sub-cluster of 'innovative approaches to construction with wood'. This potential for collaboration was considered as an essential prerequisite for successful cluster development. The second objective of this preparatory project was the development of a suitable organisational framework for future cluster development and management. In order to fulfil the objectives, all firms in the sub-cluster were interviewed and a series of workshops held.

More than 300 firms and RTD institutions with an interest in collaboration within a wood cluster were identified through this process. Together with these partners, it was possible to produce more concrete strategic key actions than in the first stage, and consequently, it was agreed to develop cluster development activities in the following five fields:

- information technology-based qualification;
- a research programme on 'innovative approaches to construction with wood';
- initiation of collaborations among firms specialising in leaf wood-processing;
- implementation of pilot projects in the cluster, in the above mentioned fields; and
- marketing and creation of greater cluster awareness.

Despite this common agreement on strategic actions, the Styrian government decided in early 1998 to reject a proposal for starting the development phase for the wood cluster, mainly for political reasons. While the Austrian People's Party, which had responsibility for economic development in Styria, was strongly in favour of further cluster development, their opponents, the Social Democrats, were reluctant to proceed as they feared the political exploitation of a potentially successful cluster development by the People's Party. The member firms of the wood cluster did not have the bargaining power (in terms of employees and output) to influence this decision.

3rd stage – definition of core projects for the cluster development. The development phase of the cluster was seen by the relevant key actors as only delayed, not cancelled. In late 1998, a third stage of cluster development was initiated. Its aim was to prepare a detailed development plan for the wood cluster that could be implemented as soon as the government decided to launch the development phase of the wood cluster.

The Styrian Department of Construction established a working group for this task. Members included representatives of PRO HOLZ Styria, Trigon, Lignum Research (a wood-related RTD institute at the Technical University of Graz), Joanneum Research and the chamber of civil engineering. In spring 1999, this working group was institutionalised as a public roundtable under the name 'Holztisch' (literally: 'wooden table'). In addition to the core group, representatives of regional cluster firms and the Styrian chamber of commerce were integrated into the process of planning.

For each of the five strategic fields that had been defined in the second stage, detailed ideas for projects and measures were prepared by the working group.

4th stage – cluster development through a sector-centred business association (PRO HOLZ). In the fall of 2000, the government finally decided to launch the cluster development project for the wood sector with a total budget of ATS 9 million (€0.6 million). It was planned that a self-supporting structure would be developed in the cluster within three years (i.e. by 2004). Compared to the development of AC Styria, a different organisational approach was chosen for the wood cluster. It was decided to hire no international consultants for the development task, instead a regional partner was appointed – PRO HOLZ Styria. In addition, an appropriate organisational structure was designed: the general responsibility for the development task was placed with the 'Holzcluster Steiermark GmbH' – a limited company with the province of Styria (26 percent) and PRO HOLZ Styria (74 percent) as shareholders. Founded in 200, this new organisation and PRO HOLZ Styria overlapped insofar as both had the same general manager.

In spring 2001, the new cluster management began its work with 18 informational workshops in the larger towns of Styria. The aim of these workshops was to create greater awareness of the advantages of a wood cluster among regional firms and stimulate a culture of collaboration among firms in the wood-processing sector. For future development, five strategic key actions will be pursued by the cluster management:

- collaboration and networks: network development and management, promotion of collaborative projects;
- human resources development at firm and inter-firm level;
- cluster oriented consulting services: benchmarking and exports;
- research and development; and
- marketing and lobbying for the cluster members.

Conclusions

Summarising the findings of the two case studies, it should be first noted that both development efforts have certain properties in common. Both clusters have been identified through empirical work preceding their development phases. In both cases the understanding of the cluster concept has been to a large extent Porterian with both thought of as groupings around highly competitive final goods. The subsequent development efforts took this mental model of a cluster into account and tried to create coherent value chains within the two clusters. In both cluster projects, a self-supporting structure for the clusters was envisaged from the beginning. The chosen development approach for both clusters has at least relied heavily in the strategy formation stage on the use of private consultants in close collaboration with members of the SFG.

Nevertheless, there are also differences between the two Styrian cluster cases. While AC Styria is today a thriving self-supporting system, the wood cluster is still in its development stage. These differing trajectories deserve a closer look at the reasons for success or failure in Styrian cluster development efforts.

Reasons for the success of the AC Styria initiative

The automobile industry might have acted as role model for the Porterian cluster: large system suppliers and car producers (the producers of highly competitive final goods) were collaborating with deep tiers of suppliers (the supporting industries). Thus the underlying understanding of clusters among regional policy-makers matched almost perfectly the structures that could be found in the Styrian automobile industry.

The cluster initiative has been launched in an industry that has been known for its proneness to organisational innovations since the 1980s. The development of AC Styria was for many regional firms in this industry just another (almost logical) step in a development that was already on-going. Just-in-time collaboration in several tiers of production and research and development projects with international partners were familiar to the cluster members and thus it was easy for the cluster managers to inspire the firms in the formation of larger strategic networks.

Styria already has had a strong regional knowledge base and innovation infrastructure for automobile engineering both in the public (universities etc.) and private sector (regional leading firms) in the forefront of the cluster initiative. Since the 1970s, this regional expertise was closely associated with international firms such as Mercedes Benz, Fiat and Chrysler and was manifested in several joint projects. Cluster development has facilitated access to this knowledge base and thus released tremendous innovation potential for the region. The attractiveness of the cluster to international investors is to a large degree determined by this knowledge base.

Reasons for the part failure of the wood cluster initiative

The wood processing industry has a highly fragmented structure and consequently, is far from being a Porterian cluster. The cluster consists mainly of isolated little networks of small and micro enterprises that are specialising in custom-made tailoring instead of flexible industrial production. In addition, there is a lack of highly competitive final goods in this cluster. New development potential such as innovative construction with wood is far from being well established in their markets and are still threatened by well-established competition such as conventional prefabricated houses. Thus, it may be concluded that there has been for the Styrian wood cluster a mismatch between the understanding of clusters by the regional policy-makers and the actual structure of this sector in Styria.

Styrian wood processing firms did not have much experience in collaborating in larger networks. Thus at the beginning of the cluster development, little willingness to collaborate and work on common issues could be found among regional enterprises. Only a few large leading firms could be encouraged to participate in these new activities. It may be concluded for future cluster development efforts that the prevailing culture in the relevant industries must be taken into account and respective analytical steps taken.

For the wood cluster, there has been from the beginning great pressure to achieve success. It was implicitly expected by the regional policy-makers that the rate of progress in the development of the wood cluster should have been as high as AC Styria. These great expectations made things difficult for the internal and external consultants already in the strategy formation stage. Thus it may be concluded that different types of cluster should also be given different amounts of time for their proper development.

Note

[22] Adamtez, Fritz and Hartmann (2000) pp.5-8.

Chapter 10

Tampere

Philip Raines

Introduction

Similar in some respects to its Nordic neighbour Sweden, Finland has been actively engaging with the cluster approach for nearly a decade now. Prompted by a Porter-style analysis of national clusters in the early 1990s (Rouvinen and Ylä-Anttila, 1999), the central government defined a policy framework detailing how cluster development would be promoted. The strategic role of clusters in the country's international competitiveness was recognised in the National Industrial Strategy in 1993, which also set the overall scope for policy intervention in support of clusters (Romanainen, 2001). The main explicit measure of regional cluster development – the Centre of Expertise programme – was controlled and funded centrally through the Ministry of Interior. At the same time, Finnish industrial policy was geared nationally to promoting the technological sources of clusters through technology development centres (such as the Finnish Technical Research Centres, or VTT, and the Technology Development Centre, or Tekes). In most respects, Finnish cluster policy has largely been dictated through the national level.

However, within these limits, regions have been able to produce cluster policies which amount to more than just regionalised versions of national initiatives. One of the best examples in Finland is Tampere region, which has not only 'customised' the national Centre of Expertise programme to form a locally-specific cluster policy, but has used the cluster approach as a powerful prism to give focus to several disparate policy measures and programmes operating at regional level. Although experiencing high levels of unemployment from the decline of its traditional industries, Tampere has strong growth centres, most visibly in the impact that the 'local' company, Nokia's rapid development has had on its emerging competences in information technology, telecommunications, software and multimedia. Around these local competitive advantages, the region has successfully produced an approach to cluster development which uses public sector resources to link together existing, rather than generate different, sources of competitive advantage.

Economic context of cluster development

Although in absolute terms, Tampere (or Pirkenmaa) is a relatively small region – with a population of only 447,000 – it is significant in Finnish terms (Council of Tampere Region, 1999). Dominated by the city of Tampere itself, it is the second largest region after the Helsinki area, and over the last two decades, has experienced a steady growth of population, making Tampere one of the major demographic growth areas of Finland. Often described as the Finnish 'Manchester' – in tribute to its early industrialisation and strong manufacturing tradition – Tampere region has historically been a significant industrial centre, especially in terms of the country's traditional industrial strengths, such as textiles, pulp/paper production and food processing.

Despite its early growth though, Tampere only ranks seventh among Finnish regions, much of which can be attributed to the region's recent industrial decline and continuing economic restructuring. As with the rest of the country, the Tampere region enjoyed general economic prosperity for most of the post-war period. However, with the Finnish economic crisis of the early 1990s, the region experienced a contraction of its core traditional industries. The national recession – arising from a combination of a global economic slump and the collapse of Finland's traditional markets in the former Soviet Union – triggered a more severe impact in Tampere (Michie, 1998). Industrial production in the region contracted by about ten percent in 1991, the unemployment rate rose to a record high level of 21 percent (higher than the national average) and employment fell faster than for the country as a whole. Since the early 1990s, economic growth has been restored as Finland adjusted to the changes in its trading markets. The country witnessed significant growth, rising to 6.3 percent in 1997 – among the highest in the OECD (OECD, 2000b) – while unemployment has declined at both national and regional levels, falling in Tampere to just over 13 percent in 2000. Nevertheless, regional economic development in the region is still based on coping with the long process of restructuring its declining industries.

The contraction and expansion effects on the regional economy have left Tampere region with a mixed industrial structure, containing sectors which are still in the process of restructuring and new economic activities which have been expanding rapidly. Traditionally, the region had the largest textile industry in Finland, accounting for about a third of the total national workforce in the sector. The impact of declining markets in the former Soviet and Eastern Europe was particularly felt in the region, with the result that Tampere no longer has any major clothing/textile firms, only a handful of medium-sized firms (Schienstock, Koski and Räsänen, 1998). Similar problems in restructuring were also faced by another key industry, pulp/paper production. As with textiles and clothing, employment in the industry shrunk over the 1987-97 period by 15 percent and is unlikely to recover its previous levels. As a result, the focus of cluster policy activity has not been in rejuvenating these traditional industries, but in newer sectors whose growth was catalysed by the region's original industrial development. Over the decades, both textiles/clothing and forest products generated wider, cluster-like developments in other industries: in mechanical engineering because of the demand for specific types of industrial machinery; in information technology through the demand for computerised automation in order to raise productivity and competitiveness; and in related service sectors supporting both the traditional and the newer industries. As it is the latter sectors where cluster policy has concentrated its efforts, it is important to review the importance of each in the Tampere economy.

As with other traditional industries in Tampere, restructuring in *mechanical engineering* led to a sharp employment decline: between 1987 and 1992, over 7,000 jobs were lost in the sectors, a contraction of a quarter of its workforce in the region (Raines, Bachtler and McBride, 1996). However, unlike the other industries, mechanical engineering showed strong recovery in output, export and employment terms, in large part due to a re-focusing of the industry on the region's competitive strengths in the production of specialised industrial machinery and automation equipment. Specialist expertise within the region can be found in mechanical and process automation, hydraulics and flexible manufacturing systems, embodied in a group of diverse companies which are significant global competitors in their fields (such as Sandvik Tamrock in mining machinery and Bronto Skylift in lifting equipment). Its growth can be ascribed to a strong continuing demand for specialised equipment in a range of industries, though the sector has also been reinforced by the strong applied research traditions in the region's universities (e.g. the Hydraulics Institute based at the Tampere University of Technology).

Nevertheless, the bulk of Tampere region's economic resurgence in recent years has principally been due to the rapid growth of its *information/communication technology* sector. Employment in the sector has increased from less than 1,000 in 1987 to 8,000 in 1997, and – at least before the recent global slowdown in the industry – is expected almost to double by 2006 (Council of Tampere Region, 1999). While initially the expansion was driven by the links between the electronics sector and mechanical engineering – particularly in automation – the main engine in recent years has been mobile telephony, both in terms of employment as well as new companies. In particular, one company has had a central role in the development of the cluster in Tampere: Nokia. Its extraordinary rise over the last decade has resulted in Nokia becoming the leading mobile telephone producer in the world and the largest privately-owned company in Finland. Tampere has benefited from this growth because of the region's traditional importance to Nokia as a RTD centre: much of Nokia's basic mobile communications research is conducted in Tampere, with specialisms in cellular and fixed systems and equipment, network equipment and software, and signal processing. This has strongly embedded the company in the region – indeed, Nokia originated in the region, though its main headquarters is based in Helsinki. While the region has not become a major production base for Nokia, within Tampere, the company employs 3,700 directly (as of late 2000) – accounting for over half of Tampere employment in the ICT sector – as well as a wider multiplier effect through the extensive use of sub-contractors.

Driven by expansion in the ICT sector, the region has also experienced rapid growth in the *multimedia* sector (Schienstock, Räsänen and Kautonen, 1999). In 2000, the sector employed 4,600, making it one of the largest service sectors in the region. It has been bolstered by a strong traditional media presence in Tampere, including one of Finland's television stations, its second largest newspaper, its first private radio station and the only university course in journalism.

At the same time, the cluster approach has also focused on a nascent competence in the *healthcare/biotechnology* field, which has developed around the research expertise of the University of Tampere Hospital. The healthcare sector in Tampere is relatively large, with 12,000 employed in region as a whole; but of this, only 1,100 are based in companies (Council of Tampere Region, 1999). The commercial sector is small, but it is its rapid growth which has underlined its importance as a potential cluster: for example, the number of identifiable biotechnology companies in the region rose from 30 in 1995 to 45 in 2000.

Origins of the cluster approach

The origins of the cluster approach in Finland lie clearly at national level. The central government was responsible for the initial cluster analyses of the Finnish economy and for defining a policy framework governing public sector interventions in support of cluster development. However, its active role in determining the boundaries of cluster policy has been mediated by the parallel trend towards the greater regionalisation of economic development policy-making in Finland. To understand the origins of the cluster approach in Finland, it is necessary to describe how a centralised national context has encouraged the emergence of regionally-differentiated policies.

National approach

The introduction of the cluster concept into industrial policy debates in Finland can be traced back to Michael Porter's work, particularly *The Competitive Advantage of Nations*. However, despite the interest generated among policy-makers, it was several years before this was translated into concrete cluster analyses and policy responses. Through the mid-1990s, a series of cluster studies was undertaken in the country, culminating in 'Advantage Finland', a large-scale project commissioned by the Ministry of Trade and Industry and carried out by ETLA, the Research Institute of the Finnish Economy (Rouvinen and Ylä-Anttila, 1999). The research made use of Porter's concepts and methodology – notably the idea of the 'diamond' for determining the sources of sectoral competitiveness – though also took into account some of the criticisms of Porter's approach (e.g. with a country as small as Finland, the researchers were forced to use 'broader' definitions of cluster in order to identify the most competitive sectoral groupings). International competitive advantage was largely identified using export data, in line with Porter's methods, and this was followed by tracing the linkages with other agents in the operating environment. The study also listed what were felt to have been the traditional sources of a cluster's competitive advantage, its *current* as well as its anticipated *future* sources. Only the forestry cluster emerged as having a clear competitive advantage at national level (or in the report's classification, a 'strong' cluster). 'Fairly strong' clusters included the base metals and energy sectors, while there were a number of potential clusters, including (at the time of the research) telecommunications and 'well being' (which encompassed healthcare technology).

In spite of the mixed results, the research provided the basis for a national policy framework for cluster development based on the concept of a 'national innovation system'. In the National Industrial Strategy in 1993, while clusters were acknowledged as key drivers in the economy, the central government declared that interventions would be limited to horizontal framework actions in their support rather than targeted preferential assistance (Romanainen, 2001). The main role of government was to provide a stable macroeconomic environment to allow clusters to emerge naturally. However, measures would be devised to deal with particular cluster externalities, of which the most significant were seen to be the technical sources of cluster competitiveness and intra-cluster networking.

With regards to technological development, non-specific RTD support has long been available through Tekes – a network of regional centres which oversees Ministry of Trade and Industry programmes subsidising business RTD – and VTT – also a regional network of government-funded agencies, specialising in applied research in different technological fields. From the late 1980s, this began to alter with the introduction of 'national innovation system' concepts which saw the role of policy in encouraging a systemic promotion of innovation. National policy responded with measures to increase business-academic networking in research across industry as a whole. This was supplemented by special inter-ministerial cluster programmes, introduced in several of the cluster areas noted in 'Advantage Finland', such as forestry, telecommunications and foodstuffs and have been designed to increase networking between businesses, research providers and government organisations. The policy shift should be seen in the context of the economic crisis which the country was experiencing and the fears that it may have been structural rather than merely cyclical. Finland's reliance on resource-based and traditional industries had been partly made possible by the economy's regional trade patterns – especially the traditional links to the Soviet Union and Eastern Europe – but the changes occurring in the early 1990s had led to an accelerated period of industrial restructuring. In order to minimise the severity of the economic depression, a cluster approach would allow for the more targeted use of resources to support Finland's competitive advantages.

Support for networking within clusters – particularly between businesses and the main providers of technological resources – was inherent in the Centre of Expertise programme, initiated by the Ministry of Interior in 1994. It was designed to "complement national innovation policy by channelling local, regional and national resources into the development and creation of selected, internationally competitive fields of expertise" (Urban Exchange Initiative III, as quoted in Brandt, 2001, p.123). The aim of the programme was to encourage the development of regional networks among the key research providers and users in different sectors. Regions would be responsible for different 'centres of expertise' and submissions were solicited from the regional councils as part of a competitive exercise.

The proposed Centres were selected using three sets of criteria: quality (such as the reputation of research in the region, the exporting performance of relevant firms and the entrepreneurial potential of the sector); effectiveness (such as the likely impact of the programme on regional development and its contribution to national industrial goals); and organisational (such as the coherence and functionality of the programme, the quality of its financing plan) (Valtonen, 1999). Eight out of 19 submissions were selected from the different regions. For the Tampere programmes, the funding provided by the Ministry was 1.5 million FIM (€250,000) routed through the regional councils, though this was matched by regional funding (in the case of Tampere region, from the municipal authorities for the city of Tampere). The initial programme was judged to have been a success, as its first five-year period was succeeded by a second round of awards and renewals for an eight-year period (1999-2006), in which central funding was raised to 3 million FIM annually.

The Centre of Expertise programme allowed a significant degree of local priority-setting and cluster selection and should be seen against a background of the increasing regionalisation of economic development policy-making in Finland. Alongside the Centres of Expertise, the Ministry of Interior was also responsible for the creation of regional councils in 1994 (Raines, Bachtler and McBride, 1996). As these councils were formed by locally-elected municipalities forming regional alliances – acting through a representative board – the change represented a shift towards decentralisation, although it stopped short of establishing a powerful regional government as the councils were neither directly elected nor able to raise their own revenue. Nevertheless, they were given key responsibilities for making regional economic strategies for the region as a whole, a task which has been given added impetus by the cluster approach embodied in the Centre of Expertise programme.

Tampere approach

Tampere region's approach to supporting cluster development has taken place within the national framework of the Centre of Expertise programme, but it has drawn on local policy networks. The approach advocated by the programme fitted in with the existing traditions of policy and industrial networking within the region, and this was reflected in the explicit objectives of the Tampere strategy. The programme document noted: "The continued success of businesses in the Tampere Region as well as their regenerating ability is, above all, based on the many-sided expertise available in the region and on cooperation" (Council of Tampere Region, 1999, p.5). In other words, the main elements of Tampere's cluster policy would be a focus on improving networking among different organisations in the region – especially enterprises and RTD providers such as university departments – as the basis for developing sustained competitiveness in three selected cluster areas at first: mechanical engineering/automation; ICT; and healthcare technology. The region's clusters were felt to have the main resources of a successful cluster (or at least have the ability to generate them over time), only not the linkages that allowed the resources to combine into a self-sustaining competitive advantage.

The Council of Tampere Region was the principal organiser of the submission, but interest in the idea was widespread in the region and commitment to participation was relatively easy to secure. The strategy for the first round was developed through a top-down approach: a coordinating group of experts oversaw the strategy development for the programme as a whole, while the individual Centre of Expertise strands were handled by separate planning groups. In the first round of the programmes, there was a widespread consensus on the choice of industries. As well as being limited to choosing a small number because of the competition nature of the programme, the aim was to obtain a selection which would reflect different phases of industrial growth in the region. The clusters would be broadly defined in order to maximise the number of companies that could participate. It was also intended that they should be complementary to ensure crossover potential between the different clusters. As a result, the strategy elected to support a 'mature' cluster (mechanical engineering and automation), a 'flourishing' cluster (ICT) and an emerging cluster (healthcare). In this context, ICT had a central role as a 'seed' cluster, overlapping with the other clusters as well as generating new clusters from within.

The strategy development for the second round did not differ substantially from the first, though it did set out a series of more precise objectives to be achieved over the eight-year period:

- to increase the total annual turnover of companies in the clusters by a factor of 2.5 and their employment by 15,000 to 45,000;
- to encourage companies to invest jointly approximately 1.5 billion FIM in their 'expertise';
- to attract more FDI to the region in these sectors; and

- to accelerate the development of subcontractors into global systems suppliers.

In the programme for the first period (1994-98), different aims underlay the three Centres of Expertise in the region. For mechanical engineering/automation and ICT, it was hoped that the networking encouraged by the programme would strengthen the value chains within the cluster. In spite of their strengths, the sectors were seen as having weak supplier bases which could be developed by supporting suppliers to become system providers for increasingly outsourcing OEMs in the region. This could be accomplished not by trying to upgrade individual suppliers, but encouraging cooperation among complementary companies. With respect to healthcare technology, a different aim drove the programme: networking was seen as a strategy for improve the visibility of the sector by drawing firms into the same geographical area (the Finn-Medi research/science park, the centrepiece of the Centre of Expertise). Such a geographical concentration would facilitate the region's potential for development in this sector by attracting foreign investment, increasing mutual cooperation among firms and encouraging access to key research providers. In the second round (1999-2006), the original three Centres of Expertise were renewed and two additional cluster areas were added: media services; and 'knowledge-intensive business services' (though the latter was only funded regionally and did not receive Ministry of Interior support).

Although the Centre of Expertise programme has been the principal component of cluster policy in the region, it should be seen against a wider background in which different sets of policies have converged around the cluster concept. Indeed, a 'proto-cluster' approach had been undertaken in the region prior to the Centre of Expertise programme, upon whose experience the region's policy-makers drew on when designing the strategy. The Tampere Technology Centre (described in more detail below) oversaw the national technology programme in support of the Finnish mobile machine industry between 1993 and 1998, as most of the major firms in the sector were based in Tampere. This programme shared many key characteristics with the later Centre of Expertise programme: it saw the improvement of business access to and adaptation of new technologies as its main objective, viewed better networking amongst businesses and research providers as the best mechanism for achieving this, and established a single intermediary organisation with the responsibility of promoting these linkages.

As well as such precedents, the cluster approach has helped to integrate policy networking and crystallise policy responsibilities among the different agencies within the region. In the design of the Centre of Expertise strategy, two other parallel strategies supporting the programme should be considered in this context: the strategy for the region's development as a whole and the City of Tampere's own strategy.

In the region's development strategy – *Tampere Region Success Strategy 2000+* – support for the Centre of Expertise programme was prominent. Indeed, the cluster concept was considerably more evident in the current than the previous strategy, arising from the Council's new role as the conduit for the programme's financing from the Ministry of Interior. The strategy acknowledged the importance of the programme to the development of the region as a whole and recognised that in achieving its goal of promoting innovation in the region, clustering was a key mechanism. The adoption of a cluster approach in the regional strategy – as one among several policy goals – reflects a development model based upon a 'growth pole' philosophy. This entails focusing regional resources on developing acknowledged expertise in the Tampere urban area. However, a key priority of the strategy was to distribute the benefits of the cluster approach through the region more widely.

The City of Tampere – through its Business Development unit – also altered its strategic approach as a result of the Centre of Expertise programme (Kostiainen, 1999). It decided to apply the cluster approach to its business development activities, recognising the need to concentrate its efforts in developing competitive advantage in the city area by making use of the Centre of Expertise programmes. In part, this reflected the importance attached to embedding Nokia's research activities within the area and the scope for the programmes to do this. The city's approach has been dominated by its strategic/funding role, in which it sets the overall guidelines and provides funding to specifically-created organisations to implement its priorities in different business areas. In addition to special companies for its property functions and venture capital arms, these 'contracted-out' organisations (in which it has part ownership) provide specific support to the tourism industry, specialist business services, healthcare technology businesses and media services.

The cluster approach in practice

In implementing the region's cluster strategy through the Centre of Expertise programmes, each of the different programmes were operated independently. As with other Centre of Expertise programmes across the country, the Tampere strategy was based on the designation of key institutions to oversee cluster policy implementation in the different sectors. These agencies were to be pro-active in encouraging networks between companies and research providers as well as in responding to networking initiatives from the sectors. In addition, the agencies were to act as intermediaries between policy organisations on other cluster issues as well.

Overall responsibility for the Centre of Expertise programme as well as specific responsibilities for the programmes developing ICT and mechanical engineering and automation were given to the Tampere Technology Centre. The Centre oversees Hermia, the region's main science park, and the core of Tampere's ICT/software cluster. Set up in 1990, the Centre also provides business support and advice to small, emerging companies based in Hermia, often supplying business idea evaluation. The Centre of Expertise programme for healthcare technology has been run by Finn-Medi Research, the equivalent of the Tampere Technology Centre for the Finn-Medi science park. Similar but specially-created agencies are operating the two more recent cluster programmes for media and knowledge-intensive business services.

As the original Centre of Expertise strategy documents were ambivalent on specific measures, each of these agencies has been given freedom to design its own programmes for supporting cluster development. In many cases, the Centres of Expertise have principally acted as conduits for other business measures in the region, providing the equivalent of a 'one-stop shop' for a particular cluster area (arguably the only effective way of maximising the limited funding for the programmes). For example, the Tampere Technology Centre has made successful use of Tekes funding to 'underwrite' joint research projects it has encouraged, effectively becoming the main interface between the public and private sector in business support for its cluster areas. However, the most significant area of activity by the agencies has been facilitating networking. Matchmaking has been a consistently prominent feature of the Centres of Expertise, either through creating fora for similar enterprises to discuss common issues, pro-actively linking businesses to university research providers in joint research projects and providing infrastructure which enables cluster networking (specifically through the Hermia and Finn-Medi science parks).

In a comparative study of the 'competitiveness' of different regions, Schienstock, Kautonen and Roponen (1999) noted that Tampere had strong RTD resources but a relatively poor track record in linking these resources into wider innovation networks to underpin the regional economy. Tampere has many of the features characteristically ascribed to a regional innovation system. These not only include government-sponsored research centres such as VTT, but also the region's education facilities (Schienstock, Koski and Räsänen, 1998). The universities (Tampere University of Technology and the University of Tampere) and associated research institutes based in the region have been a critical feature of the Tampere innovation system, because they have both generated the research expertise on which the region's main cluster industries are based and have developed efficient mechanisms for commercialising that research (often through specialised units designed to provide a research/commercial interface with local enterprises). The extensive system of polytechnics and vocational education in Tampere region has also been an important component in the innovation system by acting as a source of required skills, especially in engineering and software programming.

The networking initiatives of the Centre of Expertise programmes have played a major part in encouraging greater interweaving within the region's innovation system by linking businesses and academic research providers. They have also aimed to link the region's other major research provider – Nokia – deeper into the regional economy. Embedding Nokia into the Tampere industrial structure is widely recognised as the critical goal of the cluster activities in the ICT programme, given the company's importance as a local market and research catalyst for several of the region's clusters. The aim is not just one of Tampere cluster policy, but is indirectly reflected in economic development throughout the region.

Conclusions

Although policy is at a relatively early stage, it could be argued that Tampere region has already begun to develop successful clusters. There has traditionally been a strong existing cluster in automation and mobile machinery and more recently, the same could be argued for a mobile telecommunications cluster, with its web of hardware and software firms in a range of sectors. The strength of these clusters is not only evident from employment growth, but the presence of significant RTD centres in the region. Most of the major companies have important research facilities in the region with strong links into relevant university departments. Moreover, these are clusters that have been able to generate spin-offs into new areas, most notably in internet and telecommunications network applications and content provision. The rapid growth of a multimedia services cluster in the region is evidence of the catalytic effects of the region's existing industries.

In this respect, the significance of Nokia should not be underestimated. It has arguably been the main development engine in the region over the last few years, at least in ICT and related sectors. The speed of its growth has given the region a strong new industrial basis and focus in a mobile telecommunications cluster as well as increased the region's visibility internationally. It has been an important catalyst for cluster development in its own right, attracting investors into the region and supporting the proliferation of new ICT companies with itself as main customer. It has helped to solidify the region's technological expertise in the area through its numerous linkages into the universities. It has been a major source of skills, not least for new entrepreneurs setting up their own businesses. It has also been an important sponsor of cluster policy, as one of the funding bodies behind Media Tampere. In many respects, cluster development in Tampere has enjoyed the benefits of a happy coincidence of location: if Nokia had not been based here, the region's Centre of Expertise programmes (and their success) would likely have had a very different shape.

This raises questions about how far policy can influence the development or maintenance of the ICT cluster. If Nokia is critical to the cluster's success, its continued (and deepened) presence in the region must be a priority. But while ultimately success may depend on embedding Nokia further into the region's economic structure, it is doubtful the region can influence this greatly over the long-term, certainly given the level of resources allocated to the Centre of Expertise programme. To some extent, this problem has been partly eased by the location of many of Nokia's key RTD facilities in the region, reinforcing its commitment to a major presence in Tampere (though this has not translated into comparable manufacturing employment, as its mobile phone production is largely located elsewhere in Finland). Nevertheless, the region is restricted in its options for influencing clusters development. As a result, its cluster policy has not focused exclusively on the main drivers of its principal clusters' competitive advantage.

Instead, the policy has concentrated on creating greater linkages between the different players in the clusters. Overall, the approach to cluster development has been widely defined, including not just the region's key emerging and mature clusters (respectively, ICT and mechanical engineering/automation), but potential clusters in healthcare technology, media services and knowledge-intensive business services. The approach views cluster strength not just in terms of the presence of key competitive advantages such as Nokia, but the ability of all companies in the cluster to take advantage of the research resources in the region. Networking is central to the policy. Although its resources have been limited, the policy has targeted them on facilitating meetings between organisations on common issues, providing a broker service between businesses and research providers (especially the universities), and in several cases, supporting project development.

As an approach, it is supported by a number of factors in the region. First, there is a variety of highly active networks already present. For example, strong public sector linkages characterise the relations of its main policy bodies. Tampere is a small region, but with a relatively large number of organisations with economic development responsibilities and a tradition of personal and organisational cooperation on many issues. Recent reorganisations in the policy-making community – as, for example, the creation of the Council of Tampere Region – have further reinforced a consensus approach to economic development. Such consensus has formed around a recognition of the City of Tampere as the dominant economic force in the region and the need to favour both growth-pole and cluster-based approaches to development. It has also crystallised around the recent regional economic strategy processes, which have been founded on partnerships among the region's main policy organisations.

These policy networks made possible the adaptation of the national Centre of Expertise programme to local needs. The programme has allowed regions to make their own strategic decisions about cluster targeting and policy design within a coordinated national framework. Further, while the programme has provided few resources for policy, it has been effective in leveraging additional resources from other public sector sources. Hence, the programme has been co-funded by agencies within the region (such as the City of Tampere) and complemented by other national programmes supporting RTD development (especially Tekes, which has been critical in subsidising the research links forming between companies and research providers). In a sense, the programme has been a useful way of networking different policies and funds at national and regional level in support of cluster development.

Second, the networking approach has been facilitated by the strength and orientation of the region's research expertise. Tampere University of Technology had long undertaken research with industrial applications. Many of its units have become research cores within the cluster, such as Hydraulics Institute in the case of mechanical engineering and the University Hospital in healthcare. The University has operated within a legal and incentive system which encourages research contacts between the universities and private sector, but it has made full advantage of this through its own actions. It has organised its research activities in support of commercialisation, using institutions to simplify the contractual and legal issues of contract research and establishing units to 'front' the University's fragmented expertise in certain research fields.

Third, networking has been made easier by the supporting infrastructure of the region. In particular, the role of science parks has been critical in the creation and growth of several of the region's main clusters. In the case of ICT, Hermia has played a major role, not only in providing a geographical focus for the sector (with its proximity to the Technical University and some of Nokia's research facilities) but in projecting an image of the cluster outside of the region. Finn-Medi is anticipated to have the same impact on healthcare, and has already created a geographical concentration of the region's existing expertise.

Lastly, Tampere cluster policy has been eased by the special organisations dedicated to its delivery. Although the Tampere Technology Centre and Finn-Medi have other functions – notably science park management – their key role in recent years has been as coordinators for their clusters. Other agencies in the region have been actively engaged in the policy, through the development of the strategies for each cluster programme and in funding them, but responsibility for implementing the policy has largely rested with these organisations.

The policy appears to have been successful in the activities it has undertaken. However, despite the close fit between the design of the policy and the nature of the region's clusters, it is not clear if it will simply maximise the benefits of the existing success of the region's clusters rather than catalyse true cluster growth. The expansion of the region's clusters continues to be driven by factors which overshadow the influence of the policy. Moreover, it still leaves the region with the problem of a skills mismatch and high unemployment, as the restructuring of its traditional industries has created workers whose skills do not meet the IT skill needs of the growing, skill-deprived sectors of the economy.

It is perhaps more useful to think of the cluster approach as generating a wider policy network in support of cluster development. Already, the approach seems to have catalysed a greater sectoral focus in the economic development policies of the public sector bodies in the region. This has been most visible in the City of Tampere, which has re-designed the bulk of its business support around specialised assistance to different sectors. In this respect, the most important feature of the cluster approach is how it has informed a range of other policy areas. It has placed a priority on the setting of common, cross-region objectives for policy, tailoring support to individual sectors and concentrating resources on the most 'promising' parts of the economy.

Part 3: Conclusions

Chapter 11

Clusters and prisms

Philip Raines

Introduction

Perhaps the most common theme running through the different case-study chapters in this book is a point on which much of the research literature on clusters and cluster-related phenomena can agree: the diversity of clusters and policy responses to their development needs. In the enthusiasm for what can be broadly termed 'the cluster approach' – encouraged by the ease with which the concepts elaborated by Porter and others have fitted into existing spatial and industrial policy trends – a wide variety projects, instruments and policy strategies have been bundled together under an over-arching conceptual framework. As the chapters by Ache and myself should demonstrate, attempts to draw up single, coherent and well-defined frameworks for both cluster theory and cluster policy can only be creaky at best.

This variety is apparent not just in the scale of public sector intervention – whether measured in terms of the public resources committed to cluster development or the territorial and industrial breadth of the programmes – but also in the local philosophies governing such intervention in the first place. While cluster policies have typically evolved out of spatial policy traditions (Raines, 2001b) – evident here in the fact that government bodies responsible for spatial development sponsored cluster development in Tampere and the Arve Valley – the case studies demonstrate that this is not always so. In Limburg, País Vasco, Scotland and Styria, cluster development could be said to be part of a regionalised industrial policy, while in NRW, it has distinctly spatial as well as industrial policy dimensions. Moreover, in some territories, cluster development has been pursued as a distinctive, stand-alone field of policy activity (País Vasco, Scotland, Styria and Tampere) while in others, it has been subsumed within wider policy initiatives (the Arve Valley, Limburg and NRW).

However, while at times the cluster concept may seem like a ghost haunting different policy areas – a presence that may be difficult to define but still unmistakable – the case studies do highlight clear areas of commonality. The policies detailed here all share inspiration in the work of Porter and themes in the role of cooperative behaviour in spatial competitiveness and a multi-faceted approach to policy support for clusters. As a result, some basic concepts of cluster development have been self-consciously integrated into existing policy traditions. By reviewing the foregoing case studies, this last, concluding chapter to the book will not only consider how these concepts have changed policy design, delivery and philosophy but whether these changes can be regarded as long-lasting and even radical alterations to present policy trajectories.

The chapter has two broad sections. First, the impact of the cluster approach will be discussed in terms of the components of policy-making, characterised here as three separate and successive phases of a policy's development: 'diagnostic', 'prescriptive' and 'operational'. Second, the chapter will turn back to the question originally raised in the Introduction: does cluster policy represent a significant break with earlier policy approaches or is it merely a bundling together of existing ideas and instruments. Or put another way, is it better to describe cluster policy as a bandwagon-style 'fad', a 'catalyst' for a range of changes or a new policy 'paradigm'?

The cluster approach and the different phases of policy-making

Economic development policy – as with most policies – can be described using a life-cycle model, in which different types of activities are required at different stages of policy-making (Hogwood, 1987). This model is usually presented as an iterative process of analysis, experimentation, evaluation and adaptation. Policy options appropriate for the different stages are limited by a combination of economic needs, policy history, institutional structures, institutional and personal values and the availability of resources, acting on the life-cycle as a whole. These variables and policy actions can be modelled with respect to cluster policy, represented in stylised form in Figure 11.1 (which is based in part on Benneworth and Charles, 2001).

Figure 11.1: The different phases of the cluster policy life-cycle

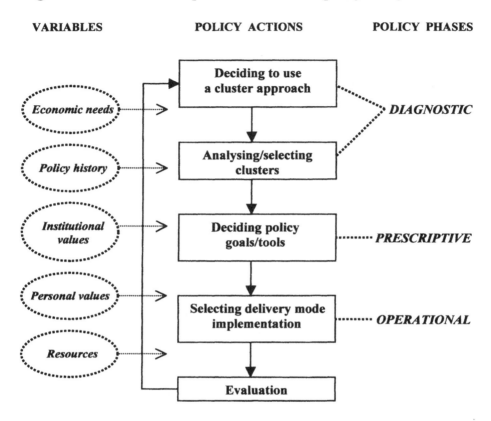

VARIABLES   POLICY ACTIONS POLICY PHASES

Leaving aside the evaluation stage – which will not be considered in detail owing to the general absence of extensive evaluation on cluster policy at the time of writing (Raines, 2001a)[23] – the life-cycle model can be used to describe three separate phases of cluster policy-making, each of which has its own associated set of policy actions:

- *'diagnostic' phase*: the stage at which the need for policy intervention – or changes to an existing policy intervention – is determined, typically comprising the decision on whether (and how) to use the cluster approach, an analysis of the economy in terms of its clusters, the selection of target clusters and identification of the policy needs of those clusters;

- *'prescriptive' phase*: the stage at which a policy response to the economic needs identified above is developed, usually consisting of the articulation of policy goals and the design/selection of an appropriate set of policy tools; and
- *'operational' phase*: the implementation stage, in which the specific policy structures and operational responsibilities are allocated and refined over the course of the policy's delivery.

With each phase, the cluster approach has interacted with existing policy approaches to spatial and industrial policy, though it is not clear to what extent cluster policy can be said to be simple variations of these other policies. To investigate these interactions, each phase is examined in turn below.

Diagnostic phase: determining the need for policy action

An analysis of the economy's needs for a new policy – or an alteration in existing policy – is the initial phase in any policy development. For all policies this will entail identifying the specific need for policy intervention and auditing the capacity of existing policy to address that need. In the case of cluster policy, such analysis typically involves a series of common tasks: determining the role that cluster development can play in either/both territorial regeneration and the competitiveness of particular industries; analysing the target economy from a cluster perspective; deciding on selection criteria for the clusters and identifying those which should be the subject of policy; and lastly, examining the needs of the chosen clusters to determine how policy can influence their development.

Cluster analysis is the first stage of developing a cluster policy. Indeed, cluster analysis and mapping techniques have been very attractive to policy-makers, even when they were not employed to develop a cluster programme. Their appeal is that cluster analysis pitches itself between two forms of economic analysis. On the one hand, it does not focus on the systemic problems occurring at the macroeconomic level, where the links between changes taking place in the economy as a whole and individual business activity are not always clear. Similarly, cluster analysis also does not treat businesses as stand-alone entities interacting with an undifferentiated economic environment, but places them in the context of their demand and input markets, often as part of industrial value chains which are not restricted to particular sectors. As well as mapping the links between different sets of businesses, it concentrates on their common sources of competitive advantage, recognising that these can be external to the firm and shared by a number of different agents in the economy (such as a pool of specialised skills or a body of acknowledged research excellence).

Another virtue of cluster analysis is that it has not been limited by traditional ways of classifying industry activity. This can be critical in understanding economic development in an environment when some forms of economic activity are changing rapidly. For example, it can accommodate the difficulties in measuring the increasing overlap between certain service and manufacturing sectors as well as the trend in some sectors for businesses to provide goods and services that feed into a range of different industries. As a result, cluster policy does not tend to be a traditional sectoral policy because the tools of cluster analysis do not define clusters around traditional sectors. While in practice there can be considerable overlap between 'sectors' and 'clusters', analysis can highlight parts of the economy which are not easily captured using sectoral analysis, as seen, for example, in the creative industries clusters in Scotland, or indeed, reveal sets of economic activities which policy can usefully support although they can be 'invisible' using traditional analytical tools, as in the case of 'knowledge-intensive business services' in Tampere.

Cluster analysis in the case studies was a two-stage process. It firstly involved the identification of clusters – in which the local economy was examined in terms of its existing clusters as well as its potential for developing them – and then the selection of those clusters to be the focus of policy. Both stages are displayed in Figure 11.2 and discussed in turn below.

Cluster identification starts the process of selecting which clusters should be targeted by policy (Stage 1 in Figure 11.2). Identification entails the analysis of the regional economy in terms of existing clusters and the potential for current groups of activities to turn into clusters with some policy support. In the case studies, it often required two types of analyses. The first is internal to the cluster: an assessment of the sources of competitive advantage in a sector, its weaknesses and the areas in which policy can make a difference. The second form of analysis is external: through benchmarking with comparator regions/clusters, determining the international importance of the cluster.

Such analysis has often combined qualitative methods – particularly local expert knowledge on the strengths of the regional economy – with an examination of quantitative indicators (such as current employment, export shares or measures of growth potential, which have been used in nearly all of the research underpinning the case-study cluster policies). In this context, qualitative analysis can be essential in identifying potential as well as actual clusters by taking into account the emerging areas of competence which have not yet been translated into measurable economic activity. Analysis is important when it also takes into account future market and technological trends which are likely to influence the international standing of the cluster.

Figure 11.2: Cluster analysis processes

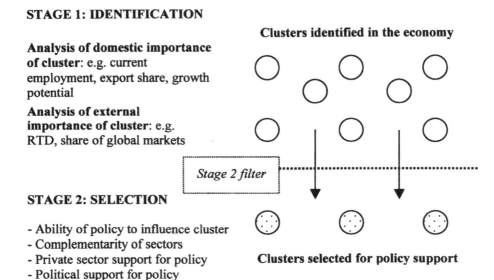

STAGE 1: IDENTIFICATION

Clusters identified in the economy

Analysis of domestic importance of cluster: e.g. current employment, export share, growth potential

Analysis of external importance of cluster: e.g. RTD, share of global markets

Stage 2 filter

STAGE 2: SELECTION

- Ability of policy to influence cluster
- Complementarity of sectors
- Private sector support for policy
- Political support for policy
- Budget limits

Clusters selected for policy support

The second stage of cluster analysis is the selection of clusters to be targeted by policy (as shown in Figure 11.2). Not all clusters identified in a region are likely to be subject to policy action. Limits may be needed because of budget restrictions and the desire to test the approach on a few clusters initially. Consequently, policy-makers require 'filters' to decide upon which clusters to act. The filters include considerations of whether the clusters can be affected positively by policy action: not all selected industries can be influenced by policy support. Moreover, the target clusters should not just reflect the economic strengths and potential of the economy, but explicitly take into account political and practical factors, recognising the importance of the cluster complementing each other and the need for widespread support for the policy in the region, especially in the private sector. In Scotland, such considerations were critical in determining the broad industrial coverage of the cluster programmes. Consensus between public and private sector has been critical here, perhaps more so than in related policy areas. Indeed, such consensus was fundamental to the approach in País Vasco, where clusters have been partially self-selecting through the emergence of cluster associations willing to enter into *convenios* with the territorial authorities.

Consequently, the cluster approach has been valued as an important analytical tool in economic development. Not only has it provided a means of understanding in greater detail the processes underlying spatial development and the sources of an industry's competitiveness (e.g. in terms of the RTD expertise of the region), it has also been an effective source of general policy information. More detailed and useful intelligence about a sector can be gathered using the cluster approach. Through the strong involvement of the private sector in the policy, up-to-date information about the state of a cluster sector and its assessment of its own needs can more effectively inform policy design.

Prescriptive phase: developing policy responses

In the developmental (or 'prescriptive') phase of policy, once the subjects of policy have been defined and their needs established, policy-makers must define the overall objectives and instruments of policy. In determining goals, policy must set limits (and if appropriate, target benchmarks) and manage expectations of what can be achieved. Moreover, in choosing the tools to achieve those goals, policy development must consider whether to use existing instruments, to alter those instruments (perhaps by changing the resources allocated to them or how they are combined with other policy tools) or devise new means of conducting policy. Cluster policy demonstrates examples of all of these approaches.

First, with respect to the goals of policy, it is important to emphasise that the cluster policies examined here are less concerned with influencing *clusters* so much as *clustering*. As Benneworth and Charles (2001) concluded in an OECD review of European cluster policies, the strategies tend to concentrate on increasing cluster behaviour within designated sets of economic activities rather than creating a well-defined cluster. Indeed, as the case studies described here suggest, there tends to be no explicit description of the set of economic behaviours which would be expected in a fully-developed cluster. Where policy goals are set, they are usually defined in terms of the economic benefits which arise from the process of clustering rather than those associated with a fully-fledged 'cluster'. The distinction is crucial to understanding the value of cluster policy when put into practice. The different cluster programmes may or may not achieve 'world-class' clusters, but the policies have common assumptions that go beyond this: they see clustering itself as a valuable economic activity.

Clustering is usually regarded (implicitly or explicitly) as closer cooperation between key economic agents in an economic activity. This cooperation takes place in ways which address market failures arising from competition but should not jeopardise the benefits of competition (through, for example, cartel behaviour). Cooperation is also not meant to exist as one-off or short-term relationships, but occur in an environment where such relationships can easily and naturally form (and terminate) without excessive friction. While policies in support of business networking and encouraging university-business linkages are hardly new, this last aspect partly distinguished the approach to network development in cluster policy: not only were linkages encouraged, but the environment for developing such linkages has been the focus of policies in nearly all the case studies. Consequently, clustering itself at any stage of a cluster's development has tended to be regarded as positive.

To influence clustering relationships and environments, the case studies produced a range of different policy measures, which varied with the differences in economies and policy structures. While they demonstrate that there is no single model for cluster policy, they display in common the view that the cluster approach is a framework for interpreting existing policy areas rather than a separate field of policy. In other words, cluster policy often acted as a way of organising a set of existing policies, making them more effective by providing better industry targeting and integration with other policies. This did not preclude developing new policy tools, but it does emphasise the clear degree of operational continuity in most of the case studies. Indeed, the cluster approach was perhaps most useful in identifying the areas where new instruments were required.

The policy tools were designed to act on different aspects of a cluster. Adapting Figure 3.1 in the Chapter 3 overview of cluster policy (and re-presented as Figure 11.3 here), these aspects can be summarised as the interactions between the different cluster agents, the collective sources of the cluster's competitiveness and the overarching sense of cluster identity. The different measures of the case-study cluster policies address at least one of these issues (though usually several) and can be classified as the following:

i.   *measures focused on specific linkages and projects*, directly promoting networking between cluster agents based around individual projects or objectives;

ii. *measures improving common resources*, supplying public goods lacking in the cluster, particularly specialised information, infrastructure and skills which would not have been produced by the cluster participants alone; and

iii. *measures promoting community building*, encouraging cluster agents to think and act as a cluster and which promote their identity.

Figure 11.3: Points of policy intervention in a cluster

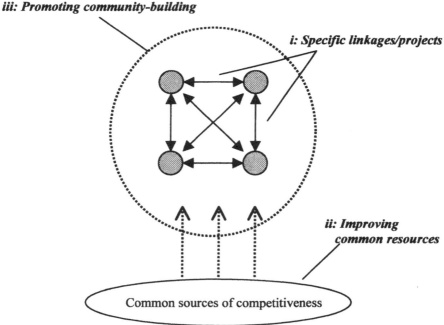

Again, the measures themselves are hardly new – though they may have been introduced for the first time as part of the cluster policy – but what mattered was their combination in influencing different aspects of cluster development. This 'holistic' approach to cluster development could be explicit in the cluster policies themselves, as, for example, in Scotland and Tampere, where all three types of measure could be found. They could also be *implicit* within a wider policy, as, for example, in Limburg, where the focus on specific linkages and projects by the region's cluster policy complemented the Regional Technology Plan within which it was placed.

The first group of measures aims to deepen the interactions between a cluster's members through concrete forms of partnership, the second creates common resources around which the cluster can develop and the third addresses the overall identity/limits of the cluster. Many policy tools have more than one purpose, and in reality could fall under more than one of these headings, but the classification does provide a useful way to structure a discussion on the typology of cluster policy instruments.

Supporting specific linkages and projects. First, measures which support networking and cooperation between the agents in a cluster are among the most common tools of cluster policy. Networking measures can involve either business-to-business ties or links between businesses and research providers. Business-to-business linkages are important in supplier development, pooling the resources of a number of suppliers in a business activity to achieve economies of scale (e.g. marketing) or improving the business performance of suppliers by encouraging transfer of experience, skills and technology. Cluster policy in Limburg has concentrated on this type of measure, particularly through the activities of the business intermediary, Syntens. In other policies, priority was given to developing the links between research providers and businesses in order to commercialise the research excellence of the region. For example, in the Finnish region of Tampere, the local Centre of Expertise and a number of university-based bodies have concentrated their cluster activity in developing business-research cooperation projects.

Improving common resources. A second key feature of most definitions of a cluster is the presence of common competitive advantages that are external to individual firms but internal to the cluster as a whole. As Chapter 2 on cluster development theory emphasised, this is particularly true with respect to tacit knowledge, whether embodied in skills or a research expertise. As a result, aspects of the case-study policies have aimed to increase that tacit knowledge through a series of measures focusing on developing a cluster's common competitive advantages. Again, the form of the measure is often not unusual, but its often highly targeted nature has been.

For the most part, such measures have been pitched at developing common resources which will improve the competitiveness of a group of firms within the cluster, but which individual firms may not have the resources or the business incentive to develop themselves, either singly or jointly. Common resources can include a variety of inputs and activities, such as access to key business information, specialised forms of infrastructure, technology transfer, tailored skills training and venture capital provision (especially for technology development). As an example of how policy has addressed such market externalities, infrastructure is discussed here.

Support for infrastructure development can be both general and highly specialised. For example, 'general' infrastructure development – i.e. infrastructure aimed at the cluster as a whole – has been a central part of the clusters in Tampere through the region's science parks. A science park has been the main focus around which the region's principal clusters have collected – Hermia and the ICT cluster – while a new science park (Finn-Medi) for the bio-medical sector has been set up for the policy to repeat these successes with a new industry. 'Specialised' infrastructure is supported in cluster policy through assistance to set up research facilities in niche parts of the cluster. They can take the form of testing or prototyping units for businesses and research providers or integrated centres of excellence, providing both access to key research and space for business development. For example, in Scotland, the Alba Centre – combining research expertise and tailored property for system-on-chip semiconductors – has been a core project within the semiconductors cluster programme.

Promoting community-building. The last set of measures has concentrated on community-building within clusters. This focus on identity was frequently innovative in terms of the spatial development traditions of the case-study regions. Usually, this type of measure had two purposes, as outlined in Chapter 3 above. 'Identity-building' could be supported through supporting the initial association of the cluster, encouraging more frequent and prolonged links between cluster members and increasing members' understanding of the cluster and their sense of 'belonging' to it. This goal was central to the cluster associations established in País Vasco. Often complementing this activity is 'identity-projecting', in which an image of the cluster could be used in collective marketing exercises or to attract foreign investors and other key actors into the cluster (as can be seen in the marketing of the 'Technic Valley' as part of the Arve Valley's cluster development).

These two goals can be seen in four sets of community-building activities which were evident in the case studies: cluster fora; communication; concentration; and branding.

- *Cluster fora.* An important part of many cluster policies was the use of regular meetings to bring together the different actors in the cluster to identify common problems and opportunities, consider joint solutions and begin to develop a wider sense of common association as a cluster.

- *Communication*. Websites and newsletters are frequent outputs of a cluster policy: apart from their ostensible goal of communication, they also help to engender a sense of common cluster identity. They can also be used to project the image of the cluster abroad, publicising the business activities of its individual and collective members (e.g. products and services).
- *Concentration*. The visibility of the cluster is higher where there is a geographical concentration of the participating firms, an important factor in being able to attract foreign investors and assist in the international marketing of the cluster.
- *Branding*. A 'brand' for the cluster has commonly been developed in the case studies. Normally part of an export development exercise, 'branding' can be used to link together the disparate parts of a cluster through common characteristics.

Operational phase: implementing policy

Policy design and policy delivery can be difficult to distinguish. In the operational phase of a policy, decisions over the specific implementation structures and responsibilities may not be easily separated from the selection of policy instruments. This is particularly the case with cluster policy, where the reliance in many policies on existing instruments has meant the use of *in situ* delivery structures, but often with the creation of specialist intermediary organisations. The result has been a proliferation of different systems. They have resulted in wholly-new bodies to deliver policy (as in NRW, País Vasco, Styria and Tampere) as well as adaptations of existing policy delivery (as in Scotland through the use of the Scottish Enterprise cluster teams) and re-designations of existing agencies as part of the cluster policy (as in the Arve Valley and Limburg). At the same time, the governance of the cluster policy showed a wide range of forms as well. In some cases, policies operated in a highly decentralised manner, as in País Vasco, where the policy has effectively been contracted out to the private sector. In others, policies have been subject to close public sector scrutiny and direction (as in Scotland).

Nonetheless, despite the diversity, two common features marked cluster policy implementation in all the case studies: the allocation of operational tasks to devolved bodies; and the strong reliance on the private sector. In both cases, while the cluster approach did not result in new features of the operation of economic development policy, it did intensify existing trends.

Cluster policy has made extensive use of devolved responsibilities for policy-making. At the level of individual programmes or projects, policy has tended to be delivered by special coordinators either drawn from the private sector or with existing close ties to businesses in the cluster. These bodies have also been effective in designing as well as operating programmes. In a few cases, new organisations have had to be set up, employing a mixture of public and private representatives. Wholly public-based agencies could be found in Tampere, where special companies have been set up with public funding to coordinate policy and deliver services to specific clusters, such as Media Tampere (for the multimedia cluster) and Professio (for the knowledge-intensive business services cluster). In contrast, the private sector has taken a more significant role in the development of several NRW clusters, notably ChemSite, a bottom-up initiative of the chemical industry. In between can be found the Styrian case, where the automobile cluster's main coordinating body, AC Styria, is a limited company with shareholding participation from both leading firms in the cluster and the main regional development agency.

The point is reinforced by the close ties between the public and private sectors in policy design and delivery necessitated by cluster development. At its most advanced it can result in the transfer of policy responsibilities to organisations embedded in the cluster – a distinctive feature of cluster policy in País Vasco, for example – but in all the case studies, cluster policy was developed out of a relatively high level (in policy terms) of consultation between the public and private sector participants in the cluster. The level of consultation and the bottom-up approach to policy delivery this encouraged was one of the clearest differences between cluster policy and its related policy traditions.

Consultation in cluster policy-making serves three purposes. First, by undertaking wider consultation, the strategy can be informed by a large body of expert opinion on the industry's trends, capabilities and needs; as cluster policy demands a highly-detailed knowledge of the industries, access to this opinion is essential. Second, consultation is necessary if the private sector is to be galvanised into taking responsibility for cluster development, particularly financially. In helping to form the policy, the private sector (and other cluster actors) will have a greater sense of its ownership and have more of a stake in working for its success. Lastly, consultation is the first step towards creating a cluster identity, whether bonding together previously disparate firms or transforming a sector-based sense of association to an awareness of a common set of competitive advantages. If the cluster is to emerge and thrive, its members must have an appreciation of their collective strengths: without this, they will be unable to identify the weaknesses in their cluster, let alone be prepared to act on them.

The cluster approach and the overall framework for policy

The review of the different stages of policy-making suggests that the cluster approach has been more critical in intensifying new concepts and forms in spatial development policy rather than as a means of introducing radically different ideas. The more targeted economic analysis, the 'holistic' scope of policy and the greater role of the private sector all represent areas where cluster policy is perhaps not so much breaking with existing traditions as making more visible certain novel features of the policy-making process. In this, the cluster approach is perhaps best thought of as a framework which combines new ideas in spatial development more 'logically' than before. Its significance is the way in which existing ideas are joined, not necessarily the ideas themselves.

In the last section of this chapter, the durability of this framework as a whole is examined in terms of the longer-term effects of the cluster approach on policy. In exploring the nature and permanence of the cluster approach in the case studies, three sets of hypotheses about the impact of the approach are considered below: the cluster concept as a passing fashion in economic development thinking ('fad'); its use as a tool in or a spark for wider changes in development policy ('catalyst'); and finally, the extent to which it can be considered a major conceptual shift in policy ('paradigm').

The cluster approach as a 'fad'

The sudden proliferation and sheer number of self-styled cluster policies cannot help but create a suspicion that there is a 'bandwagoning' element in the popularity of the cluster approach. Supported by an army of policy consultants, the approach has been proselytised globally, making it possible that the concept has been 'sold' in areas where it is not necessarily an appropriate policy for development. Indeed, with many cluster policies pursuing similar sectors – particularly in more 'glamorous' industries such as biotechnology/healthcare and IT/telecommunications/software – legitimate doubts can be raised about how many of these policies are likely to create the world-competitive clusters espoused by the policy-makers. Rather, in some cases, the cluster approach seems less a medium for regional/local economies to specialise in their existing competitive advantages than a risky strategy to develop first-mover advantages in high-growth industries – the kind of 'wishful thinking' clusters discussed by Enright (2000).

In the case studies for this volume, the question of whether the cluster approach is a passing fad is not irrelevant. For example, the issue of 're-labelling' is a real one in Limburg, where few new initiatives can be linked to the introduction of the cluster concept (and indeed, there is none of the explicit targeting associated with the cluster approach). Indeed, the concept has been specifically 'tested' in pilot programmes in areas such as Scotland and Tampere, recognition that the concept's robustness has been in need of further investigation before consideration is given to its wider adoption.

Nevertheless, in none of the case studies can the cluster approach be said to have been introduced so lightly. In some cases, it has resulted in significant changes in longer-term resource allocation and policy measures, as in the NRW and País Vasco. In regions where policy has not visibly changed in substance, the *language* of the cluster approach has still given policy a stronger conceptual underpinning, as in the Arve Valley, where it has helped to combine a series of disparate initiatives in the metal-cutting industry. Even in Limburg, the cluster concept – as part of the wider Regional Technology Plan – has been a part of a strategic framework for the Province's overall support for innovation.

The cluster approach as a 'catalyst'

In the case studies, much of the value of the cluster approach was attributed to the greater understanding it provided of the economy. By highlighting a territory's competitive advantages, it not only provides the basis for the development of a specific cluster policy, but potentially contributes to other policy areas by refining their own approaches to intervention. These changes can be direct, as with targeting, in which clusters are added as a form of additional selection criteria for policy assistance, effectively encouraging greater concentration of existing resources around specific parts of the economy. They can also be indirect, as when undertaking a cluster analysis and applying a cluster approach does not necessarily lead to a new area of policy, but results in a series of insights informing the operation of existing policies (on this point, see Feser, 1998). The question then is to what extent is the cluster approach simply a policy-making process or a clearly-defined policy *output*.

One area where this can be most evident is in the use of clusters as 'filters' for other policies. To an extent, the case studies supply evidence of some restructuring of economic development policy around clusters. While few policies are in a position to be wholly focused on cluster development – even if desired, institutional pressures would maintain other policy priorities such as social justice and more generic business development assistance – significant steps in this direction have been taken in some of the case-study regions. In NRW, the Objective 2 programme for 2000-06 have adopted cluster development as selection criteria for Structural Funds assistance, while in Tampere, the city council has reorganised its business support around specific clusters.

As a whole though, the cluster approach has largely been self-contained within specific, often pilot programmes. For example, in País Vasco, the cluster approach has not reshaped the region's wider innovation policy, which has run as a complementary, but parallel policy stream. In Styria, the approach has been successfully employed in development of the automobile cluster, but – partly because of the difficulties encountered in developing the wood cluster – it has not yet been adopted as a general principle underlying economic development. The case studies provide no significant evidence of policy resources being redistributed to favour clusters or that policy-makers would support a longer-term shift towards a 'picking winners' approach to economic development. Indeed, while several of the policies discussed here are relatively young, the evidence suggests that overall, the cluster approach has been largely explored in a policy 'quarantine'.

Signs of a more catalytic effect on economic development policy are evident not so much in the content as in the structure of policy-making. Examples of this can be found at a relatively small-scale within the case studies – such as the City of Tampere's aforementioned reorganisation of business support – but the perhaps the two clearest examples are País Vasco and Scotland. In the former, the introduction of the cluster associations has led to an extension of policy intervention at a sectoral level via a newly-developed public-private interface. The cluster policy not only targeted new areas of the economy – with its more intensive form of sectoral policy – but introduced new partnership-based forms of policy delivery for the region. In Scotland, while the cluster approach has been limited to the seven, time-limited cluster programmes, the approach has contributed to the wider restructuring of Scottish Enterprise policy tasks around horizontal objectives. This can be seen both in the new emphasis on cluster sectors in the inward investment promotion by Locate in Scotland and the greater integration of the SE network of Local Enterprise Companies around cluster development. The cluster approach does not seem to have initiated any lasting realignment of the agency's priorities as a whole, but it has accelerated continuing efforts to give more coherence to its disparate activities.

The cluster approach as a 'paradigm'

If a spectrum of policy response to the cluster approach is drawn, deepening policy-maker engagement with cluster concepts could be defined as the following line: a cursory flirtation with the ideas as a fad at one end, proceeding through a more complex, often catalytic reaction between the cluster approach and existing policy, leading to a full adoption of a new policy framework based on cluster concepts at the other end. As the previous two sections illustrate, cluster policies have demonstrated features of both the 'fad' and 'catalyst' points of the spectrum. This last section discusses the extent to which a new policy paradigm has arisen as a result of the cluster policies pursued in the seven case-study regions, and what these results may say about the policy approach to cluster development more generally.

While defining such a paradigm is a difficult task given the recent history and diversity of cluster development, the key principles underlying a cluster policy framework can still be outlined. First, a cluster-based paradigm suggests that spatial development should be skewed towards economic specialisation. While this would not necessarily mean that all policy resources ought to be concentrated in the competitive parts of the economy, it does imply more of a growth-pole approach to spatial development than is currently practiced in Western Europe. Second, the paradigm would involve an increasing desegregation of policy fields, so that measures arising from training, innovation and business development policy areas could be easily combined and tailored in support of specific clusters – indeed, spatial development policy would be reorganised so that it was less 'vertical' and (in sectoral terms) generic and more 'horizontal' and sector-specific. Third, as noted in Chapter 3, policy would target networks rather than individual firms, leading to a reduction in direct incentive-based support for businesses and a more clearly-defined role of the public sector addressing targeted market externalities within each cluster. Fourth, the paradigm would have implications for the wider delivery of policy. If the responsibility for developing policy responses to cluster development should be allocated to the level of governance at which the cluster operates, a full cluster policy paradigm could lead to greater autonomy for, and resource allocation to, regional/local public authorities. At the same time, the line between public and private sector activity would be increasingly blurred as cluster development required more partnership and close consultation. Lastly, the paradigm would have to be founded on a long-term approach to economic development, given the timescales required for significantly influencing cluster development.

In the seven case-study regions, each of these elements of the paradigm can be found, but in none of them can these principles be said to have dominated policy discourse as a result of the introduction of cluster policies. In the most comprehensive programmes, such as País Vasco and Scotland, the cluster policies are still regarded as time- and functionally-limited. Even in NRW, where the cluster approach has deeply influenced *Land*-wide debates on regional development, cluster concepts have not supplanted, only complemented existing ideas. In the other regions – and perhaps most commonly in Europe as a whole – cluster policies have taken the form of pilot schemes where the concept has proven to be a logical response to a specific and largely unique combination of policy and sectoral factors. Few regions offer evidence of longer-lasting and radical impacts. Indeed, for several of the regions here, it is not clear whether the resources and timescales built into the pilot policies are sufficient to generate the kind of dramatic economic results that would be needed to argue for a comprehensive integration of cluster concepts into spatial development policy.

The clear value of the cluster approach has been less in generating a new policy framework than in providing significant tools for making the existing policy frameworks operate more effectively. In all the case studies, policy-makers have been attracted to the cluster approach as a means of targeting and integrating their conceptual insights into local economic processes and the instruments for influencing those processes. Cluster-based analytical tools – crude as they are in some regions – have sharpened policy-maker awareness of the actual and potential sources of competitive advantage in their economies. Cluster policy development has strengthened, if not actually created new channels for policy consultation and delivery between the public and private sectors. Cluster policy frameworks have demonstrated how measures drawn from different policy fields can be combined to enhance their overall effectiveness. In effect, the cluster approach has acted as a prism in reverse – a device for bringing together different policy elements and focusing them on particular parts of the economy.

In fact, the greatest contribution of the cluster approach may be in *systematising* spatial development in the first place. The nature of the cluster concept – with its demands for a detailed understanding of how parts of an economy can gain and lose their competitiveness and for multi-faceted, sophisticated policy actions – requires policy-makers to develop a more systematic approach to analysing and responding to the local economy. It provides a ready-made but highly adaptable framework for policy-makers to examine economic development potential and their own limits in terms of realising that potential. If nothing else, even if the publicity surrounding cluster concepts fades, it will have left an important legacy in encouraging greater engagement between economic development theory and practice.

Note

[23] Evaluation in this area is an issue which has been under-researched to date, though it will increasingly become a significant aspect of cluster development policy in future.

Bibliography

Ache, P. (1994), *Wirtschaft im Ruhrgebiet. Themenfeldstudie für das Forschungsprojekt "Szenarien zur Zukunft des Ruhrgebietes in Europa"*, Arbeitspapier 123, September, IRPUD, Dortmund.

Ache, P. (1997), *Central-Local Government Relations in the Context of European Union Programmes: Case Study North Rhine-Westphalia*, mimeo, Fachgebiet Europäische Raumplanung, Universität Dortmund.

Ache, P. (1998), *Lokale innovative Milieus in altindustriellen Regionen - Theoretische Konzepte und empirische Befunde. Eine Untersuchung am Beispiel der Regionen Dortmund und Newcastle upon Tyne*, Ph.D., Fakultät Raumplanung, Universität Dortmund, Dortmund.

Ache, P. (2000), 'Cities in Old Industrial Regions between Local Innovative Milieu and Urban Governance - Reflections on City Region Governance', *European Planning Studies*, Vol.8, pp.693–709.

Ache, P. (2001), *The 'Global Economic Integration Zone' - European Spatial Planning Suspended between Image Production And Real Substance?*, Paper presented to the 1st World Planning Schools Congress, 11-5 July, Shanghai, China.

Adametz, C., Fritz, O. and Hartmann, C. (2000), *Cluster in der Steiermark. Lieferverflechtungen, Kooperationsbeziehungen und Entwicklungsdynamik*, Joanneum Research, Graz.

Amin, A. and Thrift, N. (1995), 'Institutional Issues for the European Regions: From Markets and Plans to Socioeconomics and Powers of Association', *Economy and Society*, Vol.24, pp.41–66.

Aniello, V. and Le Galès, P. (2001), 'Between Large Firms and Marginal Local Economies: The Making of Local Governance in France' in C. Crouch, P. Le Galès, C. Trigilia and H. Voelzkow (eds) *Local Production Systems in Europe: Rise or Demise?*, Oxford University Press, Oxford.

Aranzadi SJ, D. (1999), 'La Empresa Cooperativa y sus Ventajas Competitivas', *Boletin de Estudios Economicos*, Vol LIV (167), pp.271-91.

Arboníes, A. (1997), 'Unusual Concepts of Cluster: Cluster Conocimiento Experience' in *Workshop on Clusters Report*, based on an event in Bilbao, Pais Vasco 9-10 December, the Department of Industry, Agriculture and Fishing of the Basque Country.

Asheim, B. (1999a), *Innovation, Social Capital and Regional Clusters: On the Importance of Co-operation, Interactive Learning and Localised Knowledge in Learning Economies*, Paper presented at the Regional Studies Association International Conference, University of the Basque Country, Bilbao, Spain, 18-21 September.

Asheim, B. (1999b), 'The Territorial Challenge to Innovation and Endogenous Regional Development' in K. Cowling (ed.), *Industrial Policy in Europe: Theoretical Perspectives and Practical Proposals*, Routledge, London.

Aydalot, P. and Keeble, D. (1988), 'High-Technology Industry and Innovative Environments in Europe: An Overview' in P. Aydalot and D. Keeble (eds), *High Technology Industry and Innovative Environments: The European Experience*, Routledge, London.

Bachtler, J. (2000), 'Regional Policy in Europe – Which Way Forward?' in P. Coffey (ed.), *Europe – Towards the Next Enlargement*, Kluwer Academic Publishers, London.

Bachtler, J. and Taylor, S. (1997), 'EU Regional Development Strategies: Comparisons and Contrasts among Objective 2 Programmes' in J. Bachtler and I. Turok (eds), *The Coherence of EU Regional Policy: Contrasting Perspectives on the Structural Funds*, Jessica Kingsley, London.

Bachtler, J. and Taylor, S. (1999), *Objective 2: Experiences, Lessons and Policy Implications*, mimeo, EPRC, University of Strathclyde, Glasgow.

Bade, F. (2000), *Strukturelle Aspekte der wirtschaftlichen Entwicklung des* Ruhrgebie*tes*, Presentation 'Ruhr Aktuell', Dortmund.

Bellak, C. and Weiss, A. (1992), 'Einige Ergebnisse der Porterschen Clusteranalyse für Österreich', *IWI Arbeitrsheft*, 2, IWI, Vienna.

Benneworth, P. and Charles, D. (2001), 'Bridging Cluster Theory and Practice: Learning from the Cluster Policy Cycle' in P. den Hertog, E. Bergman and D. Charles (eds), *Innovative Clusters: Drivers of National Innovation Systems*, OECD, Paris.

Bergman, E., Maier, G. and Tödtling, F. (eds) (1991), *Regions Reconsidered: Economic Networks, Innovation, and Local Development in Industrialized Countries*, Mansell, London.

Boekholt, P. and Thuriaux, B. (1999), 'Public Policies to Facilitate Clusters: Background, Rationale and Policy Practices in International Perspective' in OECD (ed.), *Boosting Innovation: The Cluster Approach*, OECD, Paris.

Bömer, H. (2000), Ruhrgebiet*spolitik in der Krise. Kontroverse Konzepte aus Wirtschaft, Politik, Wissenschaft und Verbänden*. Dortmunder Beiträge zur Raumplanung, 101, Institut für Raumplanung, Dortmund.

Boyer, R. (1988), 'Technical Change and the Theory of "Regulation"' in G. Dosi, C. Freeman, R. Nelson, G. Silverberg and L. Soete (eds), *Technical Change and Economic Theory*, Pinter, London.

Brandt, M. (2001), 'Nordic Clusters and Cluster Policies' in Å. Mariussen (ed.), *Cluster Policies – Cluster Development*, Nordregio, Stockholm.

Brenner, N. (1999), 'Globalisation as Reterritorialisation: the Re-scaling of Urban Governance in the European Union', *Urban Studies*, Vol.36, pp.431–51.

Brown, R. and Raines, P. (2000), 'The Changing Nature of Foreign Investment Policy in Europe: From Promotion to Management' in J. Dunning (ed.), *Regions, Globalization and the Knowledge-Based Economy*, Oxford University Press, Oxford.

Camagni, R. (ed.) (1991a), *Innovation Networks: Spatial Perspectives*, Belhaven, London.

Camagni, R. (1991b), 'Introduction: From the Local "Milieu" to Innovation through Cooperative Networks' in R. Camagni (ed.), *Innovation Networks: Spatial Perspectives*, Belhaven, London.

Camagni, R. (1995), 'The Concept of *Innovative Milieu* and its Relevance for Public Policies in European Lagging Regions', *Papers in Regional Science*, Vol.74, pp.317-40.

CEC (1999a), *Cluster Building: A Practical Guide*, Directorate General XVI, Commission of the European Communities, Brussels.

CEC (1999b), *Sixth Period Report on the Social and Economic Situation of the Regions of the European Union*, Office for Official Publications, Luxembourg.

CEC (2001), *Enkelvoudig Programmeringsdocument Zuid-Nederland 2000-2006*, (Objective 2 Single Programming Document), Office for Official Publications, Luxembourg.

Cooke, P. and Morgan, K. (1998), *The Associational Economy: Firms, Regions and Innovation*, Oxford University Press, Oxford.

Council of Tampere Region (1999), *Tampere Region Centre of Expertise Programme 1999-2006*, Council of Tampere Region, Tampere.

Crevoisier, O. (1990), 'Functional Logic and Territorial Logic and How They Inter-relate in the Region' in E. Ciciotti, N. Alderman and A. Thwaites (eds), *Technological Change in a Spatial Context. Theory, Empricial Evidence and Policy*, Springer, Berlin.

CURDS (2000), *Universities in Regional Development*, http://www.ncl.ac.uk/unireg, visited 26 February.

Czytko, M. (2000), *ChemSite. A good place for chemical industry investments in the centre of Europe*, ChemSite standard presentation, English, version 11.0, 27 March.

Danson, M. and Whittam, G. (1998), 'Networks, Innovation and Industrial Districts: The Case of Scotland' in M. Steiner (ed.), *Clusters and Regional Specialisation*, Pion, London.

Davies, H. and Ellis, P. (2000), 'Porter's Competitive Advantage of Nations: Time for a Final Judgement?', *Journal of Management Studies*, Vol.37, pp.1189-1213.

den Hertog, P., Bergman, E. and Charles, D. (eds) (2001), *Innovative Clusters: Drivers of National Innovation Systems*, OECD, Paris.

Downes, B., Lord, J., Peters, E. and Groves, C. (1996), *Cluster Development: Taking the Network Strategy Forward*, SE(96)65, Scottish Enterprise, Glasgow.

Downes, B. and Star, J. (1999), *Future Clusters*, SE(99)57, Scottish Enterprise, Glasgow.

Downes, R., Jud, T., Sturn, D. and Rooney, M.L. (1998), *The Regionalisation of Technology Policy - International Experience and Lessons for Austria*, Report to the Austrian Federal Ministry of Science and Technology, Vienna.

Drejer, I., Kristensen, F. and Laursen, K. (1999), 'Studies of Clusters as the Basis for Industrial and Technology Policy in the Danish Economy' in OECD (ed.), *Boosting Innovation: The Cluster Approach*, OECD, Paris.

Dunford, M. and Benko, G. (1991), 'Neo-Fordism or Post-Fordism? Some Conclusions and Further Remarks', in G. Benko and M. Dunford (eds), *Industrial Change and Regional Development*, Belhaven, London.

Enright, M. (2000), 'The Globalization of Competition and the Localization of Competitive Advantage: Policies towards Regional Clustering' in N. Hood and S. Young (eds), *Globalization of Multinational Enterprise Activity and Economic Development*, Macmillan, London.

Fabris, W., Hohl, N., Mazdra, M. and Schick, M. (1996), 'Wirtschaftsleitbild Steiermark', *IWI-Studien Band*, XXVII, IWI, Vienna.

Feser, E. (1998), 'Old and New Theories of Industry Clusters' in M. Steiner (ed.), *Clusters and Regional Specialisation*, Pion, London.

Florida, R. (1995), 'Towards the Learning Region', *Futures*, Vol.27, pp.527-36.

Freeman, R. (1994), *Innovation and Foresight*, HMSO, London.

Halkier, H. and Danson, M. (1997), 'Regional Development Agencies in Europe: A Survey of Key Characteristics and Trends', *European Urban and Regional Studies*, Vol.4, pp.243-56.

Hamm, R. and Wienert, H. (1990), *Strukturelle Anpassung altindustrieller Regionen im internationalen Vergleich*. Schriftenreihe des RWI, Neue Folge, 48, Duncker & Humblot, Berlin.

Hayton, K. (1991), 'Scottish Enterprise – A Force for Economic Change', *Quarterly Economic Commentary*, Vol.16(3), pp.81-5, Fraser of Allander Institute, University of Strathclyde.

Heinze, R. and Voelzkow, H. (1991), 'Neue Politikmuster in der nordrhein-westfälischen Strukturpolitik: Regionalisierung und Korporatismus' in Institut für Landes- und Siedlungsentwicklungsforschung des Landes Nordrhein-Westfalen (ILS) (ed.), *Regionale Politik und regioanles Handeln*, WAZ-Druck, Duisburg.

Heinze, R. and Voelzkow, H. (eds) (1997), *Regionalisierung der Strukturpolitik in Nordrhein-Westfalen*, Westdeutscher Verlag, Opladen.

Heinze, R., Hilbert, J., Nordhause-Janz, J. and Rehfeld, D. (1998), 'Industrial clusters and the governance of change. Lessons from North Rhine-Westphalia (NRW)' in H.-J. Braczyk, P. Cooke and M. Heidenreich (eds), *Regional Innovation Systems. The Role of Governance in a Globalized World*, UCL Press, London.

Held, D. and McGrew, A. (eds) (2000), *The Global Transformations Reader. An Introduction to the Globalization Debate*, Blackwell, Oxford.

Held, J. (1996), 'Clusters as an Economic Development Tool: Beyond the Pitfalls', *Economic Development Quarterly*, Vol.10, pp.240-61.

Hogwood, B. (1987) *From Crisis to Complacency: Shaping Public Policy in Britain*, Oxford University Press, Oxford.

Jacobs, D. (1997), 'Knowledge-Intensive Innovation: The Potential of the Cluster Approach', *The ITPS Report*, Vol.16, pp.22–8.

Kitschelt, H. (1996), 'Technologiepolitik als Lernproze' in D. Grimm (ed.), *Staatsaufgaben*, Suhrkamp, Frankfurt aM.

Kostiainen, J. (1999), 'Competitiveness and Urban Economic Development Policy in Information Society', *Futura*, Vol.18(3), pp.14-36.

KVR (2000), *Arbeitsmarkt Ruhrgebiet - Oktober 2000*, Regionalinformationen Ruhrgebiet, KVR, Essen.

Lagendijk, A. (1996), *Spatial Clustering at the Cross-roads of Territorial and Industrial Development: A Review*. Paper presented to the EUNIT Seminar on the Territorial Dimensions of Innovation, Dortmund, 21-3 May.

Lagendijk, A. (1998), *Will New Regionalism Survive? Tracing Dominant Concepts in Economic Geography*, mimeo, CURDS, University of Newcastle.

Lagendijk, A. (1999a), *Good Practices in SME Cluster Initiatives. Lessons from the 'Core' Regions and Beyond*, mimeo, ADAPT project report, CURDS, University of Newcastle.

Lagendijk, A. (1999b), 'The Emergence of Knowledge-Oriented Forms of Regional Policy in Europe', *Tijdschrift voor Economische en Sociale Geografie*, Vol.90, pp.110-6.

Landesregierung NRW (1999), *Antwort der Landesregierung auf die Grosse Anfrage 13 der Fraktion BÜNDNIS 90/DIE GRÜNEN*, Drucksache 12/4357, 11.10.1999, Landtag Nordrhein-Westfalen.

Landesregierung NRW (2000), *Ziel 2-Programm NRW 2000-2006*, Einheitliches Programmplanungsdokument, vorgelegt der Europaeischen Kommission, Düsseldorf.

LDS (1996), http://www.lds.nrw.de/jbericht/jb_bip.htm, visited 26 June.

LEG *et al* (1997), *The Rhine-Ruhr-Region*, Düsseldorf.

Lovering, J. (1999), 'Theory Led by Policy: The Inadequacies of the 'New Regionalism'' (Illustrated from the Case of Wales)', *International Journal for Urban and Regional Research*, Vol.23, pp.379–95.

Lundvall, B.-Å. (ed.) (1992), *National Systems of Innovation: Towards a Theory of Innovation and Interactive Learning*, Pinter, London.

Maillat, D. (1991), 'The Innovation Process and the Role of the Milieu' in E. Bergmann, G. Maier and F. Tödtling (eds), *Regions Reconsidered: Economic Networks, Innovation and Local Development in Industrialised Countries*, Mansel, London.

Maillat, D. (1996), 'Regional Productive Systems and Innovation Milieu' in OECD (ed.), *Networks of Enterprises and Local Development*, OECD, Paris.

Mariussen, Å. (2001), 'Introduction' in Å. Mariussen (ed.), *Cluster Policies – Cluster Development?*, Nordregio, Stockholm.

Markusen, A. (1996), 'Sticky Places in Slippery Space: A Typology of Industrial Districts', *Economic Geography*, Vol.72, pp.293–313.

Marshall, A. (1961), *Principles of Economics*, 9th edition, Macmillan, London.

Michie, R. (1998), *Regional Problems and Policies in Finland*, mimeo, report for the European Regional Incentives consortium, EPRC, University of Strathclyde, Glasgow.

Ministry of Economic Affairs (1993), *Industrial Policy in the 1990s*, Ministry of Economic Affairs, The Hague.

Ministry of Economic Affairs (1997), *Opportunities through Synergy: Government and the Emergence of Innovative Clusters in the Private Sector*, Ministry of Economic Affairs, The Hague.

Ministry of Economic Affairs (1999), *Scope for Industrial Innovation: Industrial Policy Agenda*, Ministry of Economic Affairs, The Hague.

Morgan, K. (1996), 'Learning-by-Interacting: Inter-firm Networks and Enterprise Support' in OECD (ed.), *Networks of Enterprises and Local Development*, OECD, Paris.

Nauwelærs, C. (2001), 'Path-Dependency and the Role of Institutions in Cluster Policy Generation' in Å. Mariussen (ed.), *Cluster Policies – Cluster Development?*, Nordregio, Stockholm.

Nelson, R. and Winter, S. (1982), *An Evolutionary Theory of Economic Change*, Harvard University Press, Cambridge, MA

OECD (ed.) (1999), *Boosting Innovation: The Cluster Approach*, OECD, Paris.

OECD (2000a), *Enhancing SME Competitiveness: The OECD Bologna Ministerial Conference*, OECD, Paris.

OECD (2000b), *Economic Survey of Finland*, OECD, Paris.

Perroux, F. (1950), 'Economic Space: Theory and Applications, *Quarterly Journal of Economics*, Vol.64, pp.89-104.

Peters, E. and Hood, N. (2000), 'Implementing the Cluster Approach: Some Lessons from the Scottish Experience', *International Studies of Management & Organization*, Vol.30(2), pp.68-92.

Peterson, J. and Sharp, M. (1998), *Technology Policy in the European Union*, Macmillan, Basingstoke.

Porter, M. (1990a), *The Competitive Advantage of Nations*, Free Press, New York.

Porter, M. (1990b), 'The Competitive Advantage of Nations', *Harvard Business Review*, March-April, pp.73–93.

Porter, M. (1995), 'The Competitive Advantage of the Inner City', *Harvard Business Review*, May-June, pp.55–71.

Porter, M. (1998), 'Clusters and the New Economics of Competition', *Harvard Business Review*, November-December, pp.77-90.

Province of Limburg (1996a), *Regional Technology Plan Limburg*, Province of Limburg, Maastricht.

Province of Limburg (1996b), *Regional Technology Plan Limburg: Working Document*, Province of Limburg, Maastricht.

Province of Limburg (1998), *Regional Technology Plan for Limburg, RTP Report 1996-1997*, Province of Limburg, Maastricht.

Province of Limburg (2000a), *Regional Business Survey*, Ecos Overture Project: InterP RIS, Maastricht.

Province of Limburg (2000b), *Regional Technology Plan for Limburg: RTP Report 1999*, Province of Limburg, Maastricht.

Raines, P. (2001a), *The Cluster Approach and the Dynamics of Regional Policy-Making*, Regional and Industrial Research Paper, 47, EPRC, University of Strathclyde, Glasgow.

Raines, P. (2001b), *Local or National Competitive Advantage? The Tensions in Cluster Development Policy*, Regional and Industrial Research Paper, 43, EPRC, University of Strathclyde, Glasgow.

Raines, P. (2002), 'Cluster Development Policies and New Forms of Public-Private Partnerships' in F. Macdonald, H. Tüselmann and C. Wheeler (eds), *International Business in the 21ˢᵗ Century: Change and Continuity*, Palgrave, London.

Raines, P., Bachtler, J. and McBride, G. (1996), *An Evaluation of Regional Development Potential and Strategic Planning in Tampere Region*, Series B39, Council of Tampere Region, Tampere.

Raines, P., Turok, I. and Brown, R. (2001), 'Growing Global: FDI and the Internationalisation of Local Suppliers in Scotland', *European Planning Studies*, Vol.9, pp.965-78.

Rehfeld, D., Baumer, D. and Wompel, M. (2000), *Verbundspezifische Projekte im Rahmen einer regionalisierten Strukturpolitik. Erfahrungen in Ziel 2 Regionen. Zwischenbilanz, Best Practice und Konsequenzen fuer zukuenftige Projekte, Entwurf des Abschlussberichtes*, Gelsenkirchen, July.

Roelandt, T. and den Hertog, P. (1999), 'Cluster Analysis and Cluster-Based Policy Making: The State of the Art' in OECD (ed.), *Boosting Innovation: The Cluster Approach*, OECD, Paris.

Roelandt, T., den Hertog, P., van Sinderen, J. and van den Hove, N. (1999), 'Cluster Analysis and Cluster Policy in the Netherlands' in OECD (ed.), *Boosting Innovation: The Cluster Approach*, OECD, Paris.

Romanainen, J. (2001), 'The Cluster Approach in Finnish Technology Policy' in E. Bergman, D. Charles and P. den Hertog (eds), *Innovative Clusters: Drivers of National Innovation Systems*, OECD, Paris.

Rosenfeld, S. (1997), 'Bringing Business Clusters into the Mainstream of Economic Development', *European Planning Studies*, Vol.5, pp.3-23.

Rouvinen, P. and Ylä-Anttila, P. (1999), 'Finnish Cluster Studies and New Industrial Policy Making' in OECD (ed.), *Boosting Innovation: The Cluster Approach*, OECD, Paris.

Schienstock, G., Kautonen, M. and Roponen, P. (1999), 'Regional Competitiveness, Co-operation and Innovation – The Tampere Region in a European Perspective' in G. Schienstock and O. Kuusi (eds), *Transformation towards a Learning Economy: The Challenge of the Finnish Innovation System*, Finnish National Fund for Research and Development, Helsinki.

Schienstock, G., Koski, P. and Räsänen, P. (1998), 'The Regionalization of the Finnish Innovation System: The Case of Pirkenmaa' in H.-J. Braczyk, P. Cooke and M. Heidenreich (eds), *Regional Innovation Systems*, UCL Press, London.

Schienstock, G., Räsänen, H. and Kautonen, M. (1999), 'From Smoke-Stack Industries to Information Society: Multimedia Industry in the Tampere Region' in H.-J. Braczyk, G. Fuchs and H.-G. Wolf (eds), *Multimedia and Regional Economic Restructuring*, Routledge, London.

Schmitz, H. and Nadvi, K. (1999), 'Clustering and Industrialization: Introduction', *World Development*, Vol.27, pp.1503-14.

Scottish Enterprise (1999), *The Network Strategy*, Scottish Enterprise, Glasgow.

Scottish Enterprise (2001), *A Smart, Successful Scotland*, Scottish Enterprise, Glasgow.

Scottish Executive (2000a), *Created in Scotland: Framework for Economic Development in Scotland*, The Scottish Executive, Edinburgh.

Scottish Executive (2000b), *The Way Forward for Scottish Manufacturing in the 21ˢᵗ Century*, The Scottish Executive, Edinburgh.

Scottish Executive (2000c), *Report of the Science Strategy Review Group*, The Scottish Executive, Edinburgh.

Scottish Office (1991), *Scotland – An Economic Profile*, The Scottish Office, Edinburgh.

Shohet, S. (1998), 'Clustering and UK Biotechnology' in P. Swann, M. Prevezer and D. Stout (eds), *The Dynamics of Industrial Clustering: International Comparisons in Computing and Biotechnology*, Oxford University Press, Oxford.

Soete, L. (1997), *Zuid-Limburg als Kwaliteitsergio: Contouren voor een Nieuw Regionaal Belied*, Studie verricht in opdracht van Koophandel en Fabrieken Zuid-Limburg.

Steiner, M. (ed.) (1998), *Clusters and Regional Specialisation*, Pion, London.

Steiner, M., Jud, T., Pöschl, A. and Sturn, D. (1996), *Technologiepolitisches Konzept Steiermark*, Graz.

Stories, G. and Horne, J. (1999), 'Economic Review', *Scottish Economic Bulletin*, Vol.58, pp.5-22.

Storper, M. (1995), 'The Resurgence of Regional Economies, Ten Years Later: The Region as a Nexus of Untraded Interdependencies', *European Urban and Regional Studies*, Vol.2, pp.191–221.

Storper, M. (1997), *The Regional World*, The Guilford Press, London.

Temple, P. (1998), 'Clusters and Competitiveness: A Policy Perspective' in P. Swann, M. Prevezer and D. Stout (eds), *The Dynamics of Industrial Clustering: International Comparisons in Computing and Biotechnology*, Oxford University Press, Oxford.

Tödtling, F. and Kaufmann, A. (2000), 'Systems of Innovation in Traditional Industrial Regions: The Case of Styria in a Comparative Perspective', *Regional Studies*, Vol.34, pp.29-40.

Tödtling, F. and Sedlarcek, S. (1997), 'Regional Economic Transformation and the Innovation System of Styria', *European Planning Studies*, Vol.5, pp.43-64.

Trigon Entwicklungsberatung (1996), *Sondierungsprojekt Automobilcluster, Projektbeschreibung*, Trigon, Graz.

Trigon Entwicklungsberatung (1997), Sondierungsprojekt Holzcluster, Projektbeschreibung, Trigon, Graz.

Valtonen, M. (1999), 'The Role of the Regional Centres of Expertise in Business Networks' in G. Schienstock and O. Kuusi (eds), *Transformation towards a Learning Economy: The Challenge of the Finnish Innovation System*, Finnish National Fund for Research and Development, Helsinki.

Van den Hove, N. *et al* (1998), *Cluster Specialisation Patterns and Innovation Styles*, Ministry of Economic Affairs, The Hague.

Weiss, A. (1994), 'Österreich als Standort international kompetitiver Cluster', *IWI-Studien Band*, XIII, IWI, Vienna.

Wever, E. and Stam, E. (1998), 'Clusters of High Technology SMEs: The Dutch Case,' *Regional Studies*, Vol.33, pp.391-400.

Wintjes, R. and Cobbenhagen, J. (2000), *Knowledge Intensive Industrial Clustering around Océ: Embedding a Vertical Disintegration Codication Process into the Eindhoven-Venlo Region*, MERIT, University of Maastricht, Maastricht.

Yuill, D., Bachtler, J. and Wishlade, F. (eds) (1999), *European Regional Incentives 1999*, 18th edition, Bowker-Saur, London.

Index

For Product Safety Concerns and Information please contact our EU
representative GPSR@taylorandfrancis.com Taylor & Francis Verlag GmbH,
Kaufingerstraße 24, 80331 München, Germany

Printed and bound by CPI Group (UK) Ltd, Croydon, CR0 4YY

01/05/2025

01858342-0008